SILENT FIRE

SILENT FIRE

Bringing the Spirituality of Silence to Everyday Life

James A. Connor

Crown Publishers
New York

Grateful acknowledgment is made to the following for permission to reprint previously published material:

Adele Kenny: "moonrise," from *Castles and Dragons* (Yorkshire House Books with Muse-Pie Press, Passaic, NJ, 1990), copyright © 1990 by Adele Kenny; reprinted by permission of the author.

Alfred A. Knopf, a division of Random House, Inc.: "The Idea of Holy" from ON LOVE: POEMS by Edward Hirsch, copyright © 1998 by Edward Hirsch. Used by permission of Alfred A. Knopf, a division of Random House, Inc.

New Directions Publishing Corp: "Of Being" by Denise Levertov, from OBLIQUE PRAYERS, copyright © 1984 by Denise Levertov. Reprinted by permission of New Directions Publishing Corp.

Published by Crown Publishers, New York, New York.
Member of the Crown Publishing Group.

Random House, Inc., New York, Toronto, London, Sydney, Auckland
www.randomhouse.com

CROWN is a trademark and the Crown colophon is a registered trademark of Random House, Inc.

Printed in the United States of America

Design by Susan Maksuta

Library of Congress Cataloging-in-Publication Data
Connor, James A.
Silent fire : bringing the spirituality of silence to everyday life / James A. Connor. —1st ed.
1. Silence—Religious aspects—Christianity. 2. Spiritual life—Christianity. I. Title.
BV4509.5 .C659 2002
248.4'7—dc21 2001032504

ISBN 0-8129-9102-8

10 9 8 7 6 5 4 3 2 1

First Edition

Author's Note

Writing out of twenty-year-old memories is like watching black-and-white home movies. Things jump around, and people are never quite as they once were. Though I have tried to pound accuracy into these memories, I was only partially successful. Moreover, I have taken a few liberties with the details when they involved the sensitive parts of other people's lives, and I have disguised the identities of several of them because I believe in their right to privacy. No one will ever know the identity of the mother whose child was killed. Courtesy, at least, demands this.

By way of dedication, I include this list:

Reverend John McDougal
Michael Gurian
Reverend Raymond Deviney
Thich Nhat Hanh
Mary Mondello
Marian Cowan
Reverend James McCawley
Archbishop Adam Exner, O.M.I.
Lou McCabe, S.J.
Michelle Marie Connor, O.C.D.
Gerald May

And all those working in the field.

In Appreciation

There are many people who have made the long walk of this book possible. First, Elizabeth Rapoport, Stephanie Higgs, and Luke Mitchell, my editors at Crown, for their talent, professionalism, and endurance. Next, Giles Anderson and Daniel Baror, my agents, for all the good stuff that agents do. Jerry Bauer for the photographs, Michael Gurian for the good advice, Charlie De Fanti and Leni Fuhrman, Robert and Nancy Cirasa, Susanna and Morton Rich for their reading and feedback. N. Scott Momaday, William T. Craven, Gerald May, Avis Meyer, and Kathleen Corkery-Spencer for their friendship and encouragement. My colleagues at Kean University, who suffered through the ups and downs of the writing process. The Benedictine fathers and brothers at St. Meinrad's Archabbey, the fathers and brothers of the Oregon Province of the Society of Jesus, and the Zen teachers that I have encountered over the last twenty years. My parents, John and Margarette Connor, for peppering me with questions; Archbishop Adam Exner of the Archdiocese of Vancouver, Canada; all of the great spiritual teachers, East and West, whose ideas have formed me. Finally, I would like to thank my wife, Beth, for being my first reader and primary sounding board.

Contents

THE IDEA OF THE HOLY

Out of the doleful city of Dis
rising between the rivers

Out of the God-shaped hole in my chest
and the sacred groves of your body

Out of stars drilled through empty spaces
and Stones in My Passway at four A.M.

All those hours studying under the lamp
the First Cause and the Unmoved Mover

the circle whose circumference is
everywhere and whose center is nowhere

the Lord strolled under the oak tree at Mamre
at the hottest moment of the day

the Lord vacated a region within himself
and recoiled from the broken vessels

a God uncreated or else a God withdrawn
a God comprehended is no God

Out of subway stations and towering bridges
Out of murky waters and the wound of chaos

Out of useless walks under fire escapes
Be friends to your burning

I saw the sun convulsed in clouds
and the moon candescent in a ring of flame

souls I saw weeping on streetcorners
in a strangeness I could not name

O falling numinous world at dusk
O stunned and afflicted emptiness

After three days and nights without sleep
I felt something shatter within me

Then I lay down on my cot motionless
and sailed to the far side of nothing.

EDWARD HIRSCH

Prologue in New Mexico

The Night and the Comet

I was a priest once—a good one, by some accounts. My entry into the priesthood is one part of the story; my exit is another. I trace the first back to one event, which happened five days after Christmas. A blanket of snow had drifted onto the desert; it was 3:00 A.M. and I was bopping a yellow 1970 Ford Maverick along Interstate 10 just outside of Lordsburg, New Mexico. The Milky Way straddled the sky, a silver band speckled on the black; the stars were so bright I could almost hear them hum. I was sipping my fourteenth cup of coffee—three thermoses and two truck stops into the night—when I topped a rise on the farther outskirts of Lordsburg and saw a comet hanging in the sky, silver blue, as if someone had taken a brush and dabbed it on, one stroke, just above the horizon.

At that exact moment, I was deep into Crosby, Stills, and Nash, Woodstocking my way along, driving with my knees, taking a sip of coffee, then beating out the time on the dash with my fingers. I was singing "Marrakesh Express" at the top of my voice, in eleven or twelve different keys, when I saw the comet. Because it was the early 70s, I pulled the car over and said, Whoa! Yeah, man! and poured myself another cup of coffee. I stopped the engine and the music died, the beat ebbing slowly, as if the echo of its sound inside the car and inside my head took time to quiet. Sipping, I stared out the windshield at the comet, something I had never expected to see, whose name I have never since discovered. It seemed huge, partly because of the darkness of the sky, partly because of the fourteen cups of coffee, and it seemed dream-like, an image that appeared ex nihilo, out of nothing, as if the laws of science had suddenly softened into mere guidelines.

Silence enclosed me. At first, I felt it as emptiness—the loss of the music from my cassette machine, the loss of engine noise, the loss of wind against my car. Gradually, the stillness grew palpable, came alive. I opened the door and got out into the cold. The snow glimmered in the night, as if starlight had saturated the ground and was evaporating into the air. I inhaled deeply and felt the inward pull of my breath, slipping with the rise and fall of it into a more profound state of peace.

Holy, Holy, Holy
Is the Lord God of Hosts!

I found myself whispering over and over, drawing further into the thickening silence until soon, the head babble of fears, hopes, desires, regrets, depression, elation, stupid ideas, half-formed thoughts, strange hunches, all hushed, until I was as quiet inside as the white glowing desert around me, as quiet as the softly pulsing stars and the comet still hanging two inches above the horizon.

At last I lost all thought of myself. I lost the sense of myself watching myself, and was just there as the desert and the comet were there with the stars, the cold, the stinging in my cheeks and my nose, the warmth of the hood on my buttocks, the heat of the coffee cup in my hand. The hall of mirrors we call consciousness had opened, and I no longer found myself doing anything, because I was no longer looking, even surreptitiously, at myself.

Halfway through a single breath, the night revealed itself as joy. The joy did not rise up from me, nor was it in me—or if it was in me, it was only because I was in the night. It was more than a feeling; it was an understanding, a knowledge beyond words. Joy resonated like a struck bell. It was a presence, something that had been there all along, if only I had been aware. Would I call it God? Perhaps, but I could also call it by a million other names, and it wouldn't matter, because finding the right name for it is beside the point. It is unnamable; it exists outside of words, part feeling, part perception of the true state of affairs. It is an insight, a quick realization that there is no me and no not me; no inside me and no outside me, but only one ineffable reality. A bubble of laughter tickled my chest, and I wanted to dance like Zorba the Greek at three in the morning beside a highway in the New Mexico desert. I raised my hands, snapped my fingers, and did a little turn. I shuffled my feet in the snow and did another turn, and immediately thought about how ridiculous I looked, hoping that a truck didn't happen by and see me. And as that stray thought nested inside my head, joy retreated as if it were offended. I stopped dancing and sighed deeply, poured myself another cup of coffee, leaned back against the hood of the car, and watched the comet until dawn.

The rest of my life has been spent trying to find that joy once again.

The heart of the spiritual life is the shattering apprehension that my life is not necessary, that there are no laws of nature insisting on my existence, that I am a bare fact, and that fact, because it is a fact, is a mystery. My life is a gift, as is the life of every other Jack and Jill who luxuriate in existence. Vietnamese Buddhist master Thich Nhat Hanh says that life is a miracle, and that each moment in life is a miracle. Anyone who can feel that, who can know it to be so, moment to moment, is a spiritual person. The rest of us are travelers on the way, watching for signs, landmarks to the next miracle. This is a journey inward, and silence is the landscape we travel through. In that land there are four circles nested one into the other like the rings of trees, each penetrating further into the ego, the false self. The traveler moves deeper from one silence into the next, first abandoning words, then stilling the soul, then losing self-consciousness, and, finally, embracing the world as it really is, not as we dream it to be. It's not easy going. A wall separates each circle from the next, and the gates leading from the outer circles to the inner get narrower each time. By the last, you are on your belly, crawling like a soldier under fire. At each gate, like the camel crawling through the eye of the needle, you must abandon something, something you were sure you absolutely had to have but really didn't need. The journey from circle to circle is the journey of an entire life. In meditation, it will be manifest as a state of relaxation and a state of activity, forever a balancing act between sleeping and waking. In life, it will form a daily practice that will permeate all your actions until one day you will feel unspeakable joy while standing at the bank waiting to write checks.

You may break into new territory in just a few minutes, as if your entire life had been jockeying for this moment, and you will find yourself suddenly open to the world, and the world suddenly open to you. Most times, however, you will struggle through each condition, sometimes for years, making scant headway, then falling back again. Exploring the circles is a poet's life—you practice every day, bleeding on the page until one day out of the blue the words flow and the writing is holy.

THE FIRST CIRCLE OF SILENCE

You enter the first circle when you decide to invite a bit of silence into your life. You may do this deliberately as part of a plan to achieve spiritual perfection and greatness of soul. Or you may be thrown into it bodily as I was, forced into it by life. Either way, you've likely already made a thousand false starts. You're all too familiar with the obstacles to getting on your way—your friends call, the kids need to be picked up and dropped off, the office needs that report by Friday. You tell your friends that you're about to set off, hoping they'll understand, but instead they worry. And when you do finally make a break for it, suddenly there you are, alone, in the stillness of your room, or on a retreat, or in your car, and you find that you notice you need to wash the car. You need to scrub behind the refrigerator. The ceiling fan needs dusting. Never have such distractions seemed so urgent. You're trying to meditate, and suddenly you are hemmed in by the flotsam of memory—like an old woman who throws nothing away, you find that your mind is full of junk. You thought your memory was a sieve, but after five minutes you realize that you've forgotten nothing. You haven't left the noisy world behind, you brought it with you inside your head. My brother once said that the problem with running away from yourself is that you have to take yourself along to do it.

The watershed of my spiritual life emerged soon after I entered the seminary. I first studied with the Benedictines in southern Indiana, and until that time prayer had been a monologue. I talked, God listened. I whined, God listened. I treated God the way I treated my parents—I asked for things. On one autumn evening in my first year at the monastery, I was sitting outside the abbey church on a concrete bench watching the stars as the monks chanted Vespers inside, and in that silence I found enough peace to truly pray for the first time in my life. In that one evening, I discovered meditation. Surrounded as I was by monks and bells and prayer and the green hills of Indiana, I was in the perfect place to learn.

Sometime later that year, I discovered the writings of Thomas Merton and eventually wandered into his Asian journal. Here, I thought, is religion at its core, the estuary where spiritual rivers come together and blend with the sea. From that time on, through all my years as a Jesuit, I studied both Western and Eastern meditation. One week I read *The Cloud of Unknowing;* the next week I read the Buddha. Studying both Christianity and Zen Buddhism at the same time made me giddy with freedom. Before I was born, my mother had converted from the Southern Methodists to the Catholic church, declaring religious war on her family, and they on her. All my life, I had been forced to relive the Reformation and the Counter Reformation. Many times, I had nearly despaired of organized religion, because it too often seemed to be a place of war. As I grew in meditation, however, I realized that all of those theological disputes were the products of frightened human beings, men and women too afraid to love. Authentic religion, I realized, should lead to that estuary where spiritual traditions blend, where monks in saffron robes chant side by side with monks in Benedictine black. That realization led me to the first circle, which is the place to throw things out, to clear away the mess, and see things anew. It is the place that Merton calls "solitude." This is the place of detoxification, where you throw away your old furniture and wait for the new stuff to arrive. All the while, your house feels empty. In the first circle you concentrate on your inner life, on your breathing, your thoughts and your feelings. You step out of human society for a time. You go it alone, find solitude, and, simple as it sounds, you learn to breathe.

But the world of noise and busyness prefers your company and wants you back. Now it's inside your own head, the voice that you think is "you," telling you to work, buy, sell, run, talk, talk, talk, talk! We are all possessed by a million chattering spirits, the spirits of television and radio, of our parents and teachers, of our bosses and coworkers, telling us to buy Pepsi, sit up straight, eat our peas, get our book reports in on time, and respond to that memo by tomorrow. We have little slips of pink paper with phone messages on them, dunning letters from the gas company, e-mails from the stockbroker, and everyone wants our complete attention. If you were to take all the things you were expected to respond to in a single day and pile them up, you might disappear behind the pile. And we wonder why we are in a constant state of stress.

THE SECOND CIRCLE OF SILENCE

The second circle begins at the moment you decide to confront the inner noise churning away inside your brain, the junk left over from the active life. You have passed through the initial anxiety, the initial fear of emptiness, the fear of the loss of human society, and have learned to desire the silence—not just in the abstract but in its immediate presence. This is hardest for extroverts like me. Whenever I take the time to be silent, I quickly become depressed. The sudden loss of stimulation is a shock; I feel it as a drop in energy, even as I move from one level of relaxation into the next. When I was ten, I used to be afraid that if I relaxed enough, I might keep on going, deeper and deeper, and never be able to find my way back. Relaxation seemed too much like the vestibule of death to suit me, and I wanted to run and run because I feared that I might die if I stopped. The second circle emerges from a similar fear. If I truly stop doing, running, acting, thinking, then will I stop being?

The second circle is the place of inner silence. There are distractions here, too, as if the noise of daily life gets shoved inside your head. The key to this circle is that when a stray thought crosses your mind, when a distraction hits you, you let it pass. This is not as easy as it sounds. In the fourth century, people by the thousands left the cities of the Middle East to live in hermitages in the mountains of Turkey and Greece, and in caves in the vast deserts of Egypt. All of these people, men and women, left their homes in search of silence. The most noteworthy of these were the Desert Fathers and Mothers who lived in a place called Scete, near the Nile River valley, and who eventually passed down to us a ream of lovely stories. In one, a young monk goes to the abbot and complains that when he meditates in his cell, he is besieged by distractions, and when that happens, he just doesn't know what to do with himself, and that his days seem terribly long. The abbot tells him that this is to be expected, that he has spent his life like someone living in a city square with his door open as an invitation to people to come by and chat whenever they want. "Now," said the abbot, "you have closed your door, and the same people are coming by and wondering if you are all right. They are knocking on your door, sometimes pounding to get in. If you open the door to them, they will never go away, but if you wait there in silence, eventually they will tire, and leave on their own, and you will be left in peace."

Somewhere in this second circle, you begin to discover that you are not your thoughts any more than you are your activities, or your possessions, or your fears or your dreams. You will discover that you are something else, an awareness that sits abandoned in the middle of a bus station of noise, forgotten in the hubbub, increasingly lonely, increasingly afraid. Even your thoughts are a kind of noise that keeps the awareness, the self that exists below and beyond words, distracted and bemused.

THE THIRD CIRCLE OF SILENCE

The third circle begins when you turn your awareness away from yourself and lose yourself in the world around you. You may have experienced this already. Any good athlete knows the moment when she hits the sweet spot, the golden moment when her struggle, her pain, her fears go forgotten, and the whole of her flows through that moment. I play classical guitar, and I have this experience all the time. I practice endlessly, hating all my mistakes, and then one morning I pick up the guitar and the piece plays itself, and I am utterly taken up in the music. In this circle, you forget to watch yourself, forget to evaluate your thoughts, your actions, your dreams, you forget to compare yourself with other people, to ask how you measure up, or whether you are good enough. The third circle is the place of true forgetting, where eternity begins, the ever-present now that has no past and no future, only an awareness of what is here, now, in this instant. The third circle is both the hardest and the easiest to achieve, because on one hand, you cannot force your way into it. The more you try to force it, the more self-conscious you become ("Are we there yet?") and the more self-conscious you are, the farther away from this circle you will be. And yet, the moment you stop trying, the moment you surrender the attempt, is the moment it happens. Like love. Drives you nuts.

THE FOURTH CIRCLE OF SILENCE

The fourth circle is what Thomas Merton calls "contemplation." For Merton, contemplation is the highest expression of the human intellect and the spiritual life, an expression that pulls together the entire person and goes beyond rational consciousness. It is "That life itself, fully awake, fully active, fully aware that it is alive." Contemplation is, as Merton says, "spiritual wonder." For this reason, the fourth circle is not really in our control at all; it transcends all technique, all processes, all decisions on our part, and happens when it happens. Contemplation is the fullest expression of what we mere humans are, a connection between something higher and ourselves, an opening to God.

At the core of every human soul is an imperishable flame, the same energy that permeates all things—the fire of the comet, the twinkle of the stars. Like a campfire broadcasting light in wide circles, that flame illuminates the world, and as I move inward in silence, the world brightens. The difficult part is that I must make that journey alone. Armies of priests, preachers, therapists, and masters can only stand outside the circle and attend, because the way to the fire, the way into my own soul, is a solitary way, a silent way.

Exploring the landscape of silence is the point of life. It is why we are here. It doesn't take a near-death experience, nor does it take a great trauma, nor does it take years of renunciation and suffering, nor fourteen cups of coffee and an astronomical event, though each of these may be a doorway into it. It takes a simple moment of attention and receptivity, a moment that sometimes feels accidental, as if you happened upon it, as if you turned a corner and it was there, though your whole life has been a preparation for it. What made that moment different, there in the night against the hood of my car, in the whisker-thin instant between being in the silence and stepping outside of it, I took note, remembered it, saw it as important.

A friend of mine once told me that she had had a similar experience while sitting on a hillside overlooking a small lake. She was just a young girl at the time, no more than twelve, and she found herself relaxing in the caress of a summer breeze against her face, the sounds of crickets all around her in the brush, the call of a bird, the sun setting red through the mists hanging above the yellow water. At that moment, she said, she felt herself to be a part of everyone on earth, connected somehow in a great dance, each a part of each, all connected to all. Now, she says, nearly fifty years later, she meditates as often as she can, and watches every sunset she is able to, hoping to catch a glint of that first experience. From time to time, she succeeds, and the world opens up for her for a few minutes of wonder—then it closes back again, as if she were only capable of taking in such glory a bit at a time.

The experience changed her irrevocably. It has never let her spirit fall back to sleep, but it has kept her aware of the world around her in a way that few others are. Once, we were walking along a hillside, and as the sun set, she began hopping up and down like a little girl, pointing out the colors she could see in the sky: a touch of mauve, a hint of yellow, a splash of gold, as if that sunset contained all the colors in the world, the full spectrum of passion, from joy to sorrow. Are these religious moments, or are they moments of aesthetic awareness, an awakening to beauty? It is hard to say, really, because the experiences of mystics and of poets have never been far apart. Perhaps beauty is a momentary sheen off the face of God.

What we call religion is something else again, however, and stands to the world of mystics in the same relation as universities stand to the world of poets. The word "religion" comes from the Latin *religio*, which means "an ordered practice," or an "activity leading to the perfection of some human quality." To say that a football team practices religiously is not really a metaphor. But such practices may demand institutions, like the NFL, to organize and protect them and to promote their lifestyle within the wider society. People find a way of life that is beautiful, and then they build a building to protect it, and then collect all manner of odd notions about it, making the building into a curiosity shop of wondrous truths, old ideas, and silly notions.

So the thing we call "religion" is an official protector and promoter of the experience of silence. Psychology is another. In either case, the actual experience is its own justification, and while the institutions that we build around it can be helpful to us in locating the silence we need to achieve the experience, they cannot claim to own it, for what we find in silence cannot be owned. Buddhists call it dharma, the liberating truth of nature. Christians call it the Face of God. We can pursue this silence within the structure of religion or without it.

In this book, I'll share with you my journey into silence. But language has its limits. When people ask me "What do you mean by this?" sometimes the only thing I can say is "Go and find out for yourself."

Soon after the comet, I took a Zen retreat in Portland, Oregon, and because I was young and cocky, and thought I was very funny, I asked the master what the sound of one hand clapping was. He nodded thoughtfully, stood up, walked over to me, and without ever breaking a smile, slapped me smartly across the face. The answer: Don't ask stupid questions. Go and do. Find out for yourself, because words cannot contain what you will find. "Eye has not seen, nor ear heard . . . ," said Saint Paul (1 Cor. 2:9).

Like a slap in the face, like a fire in the night sky, I had to be thrown into silence, because I had resisted it for so long. A bright light had been cast into a shadowy room, and for the first time, I could see what was there. Silence the revealer gives light to the eyes of the blind and opens the world to the soul. The night, then, is revealed as joy.

I

The First Circle of Silence

No Words

moonrise:
at the edge of the woods
we listen

Adele Kenny

One

THE BACK DOOR TO the hospital shushed open and I turned the corner into the emergency room, which smelled of alcohol, fresh linen, and old wounds. Fluorescent lights fluttered like ghosts, heart monitors beeped sadly, a nearby patient's respirator wheezed, while the nurses tended patients, moving quietly, speaking softly, though no one looked at anyone else. Continuing down the hall, I approached the outer nurse's station where Heather the candy striper sat sorting papers. I waved and called her name, said hi, but she looked at me as if she were about to burst into tears over something I didn't know I had said. I looked at her, puzzled, and then felt it—a tension in the room, a free-floating fretfulness. A young blond nurse, new to the business, shot me a quick, angry look, and then embarrassed, looked away.

At the emergency room nurse's station, Anne was vehemently typing out a form. She was forty-two, dark-haired, trim, had three children and a husband who was a pediatrician, a Presbyterian fellow who liked to tell me pope jokes. When she looked up and saw who I was, she gave me that same angry look.

What's with everybody today? I said.

Anne glanced at a closed cubicle at the back of the room. I looked, puzzled, and started toward it, but she reached over the desk and grabbed my arm. You can't go back there, she said. You don't know what's happened. Instead, she led me into the hallway.

A young couple is in there, she said. *Very* young, she said. They just had their first baby.

Okay, so?

Just listen. Anne was looking at the floor, trying to gather herself.

They were on a road trip, she said, as if explaining to a child. They were bringing the little girl home to meet her grandparents. Both families were waiting for them. A big *party* and everything, Anne said, pulling a curl of hair off her face with her fingers.

They buckled the baby into a safety seat. And they turned the seat backward, you know, so if there was an accident . . . Anne paused.

They did *everything right!* she said, a catch in her voice.

So what happened? I said.

They were driving through a canyon on their way to their parents . . . And a rock fell off the cliff and hit the back of the car. A big rock.

Oh . . . , I said.

They were fine. Not a scratch. But the rock crushed the baby to death.

I looked toward the back of the emergency room, knowing what I had to face. The fluorescent lights flickered; a heart monitor beeped; the nurse moved from one side of an old woman's bed to the other, took her wrist, and stared at her watch.

Jesus, I said.

Reality is a leaky boat. Take enough of a hit and you get your feet wet. You vaguely feel the world around you, the fullness of the air in your lungs, the beating of your heart, the tug of the jacket on your shoulders. You see people, you see faces; but rationality recedes and the world feels as it does half a second after waking—vague, discontinuous, the intimation of a dream world fading. The faces stare, the faces of the nurses wanting something, a word, anything. Say something. Make sense of this for us. But there was nothing to say. For the first time in my life, I was shocked into silence.

Everyone in the emergency room was watching me as I drew aside the curtain and crabwalked through the slot. As the resident priest, with nothing left for modern medicine to do, I was expected to step in. The couple was sitting side by side next to a hospital bed with chrome side rails. He held her hand, but she stared straight ahead. The baby was in the morgue, but her absence was like a smell that lingered. The mother sat still. The father fidgeted, whispered something to her, but she just stared, like someone who'd been shot in the head and was trying to figure out what had happened. Her mouth worked several times, but aimlessly, half speaking, half chewing, as if it had become disconnected from her brain. One hand lay limply in her husband's hand; her other hand clutched her blouse. Her breasts did not yet know there was no longer a baby to nurse. Sitting so attentively next to her, her husband was trying to find something to say, even something stupid. He wanted to *do* something to keep this terrible nothing at bay. He held her hand, then whispered, then turned away, boiling up a new plan, then back again, all his energy and good intentions falling into the empty crater of her grief. Pulling slightly away from her husband, she lay her head on the cool chrome of the bed and shut her eyes, bent over like an old woman.

For the next two hours, because it was my job, I sat with them, my mind turning over ideas, things to say. I could talk about the love of God, but I might burst out laughing, that mad laughter you see in movies. Then I thought, What about the death of Jesus and the suffering of Mary? And then I thought, Who wants to hear about the suffering of Mary when they have enough suffering of their own? And then I thought, What about Purgatory and the perfection of the soul through suffering? And then I thought, If this is perfection, you can keep it. And then I thought, Maybe the baby had to die to serve some larger plan we can't see. And then I thought, How could God's plan possibly be served by the death of an innocent? And then I thought, Maybe God knew something about the baby we don't. And then I thought, What? Blame the baby? Explanation after explanation, each more horrible than the last, marched through my head like picnic ants, a psychotic marching line of platitudes and infernal metaphysics, an Escher print of theological tomfoolery, while my thoughts beat like a butterfly in a mason jar. All that theology and yet nothing made sense. My head hurt.

Across the room, the father rocked back and forth like a child with a bellyache, then looked at me, still rocking, desperation in his face. I took off my glasses and rubbed my eyes. All my words had left me; I was a shell of silence. I had been emptied out. I leaned forward on the folding chair, the heels of my hands pressed against my eyes. No more answers, no more easy responses, no more fast-draw, shoot-from-the-hip explanations of life. I had no comfort to give, because there was no comfort to give.

The father stood, sat down, rubbed his hands across the top of his thighs, stood again suddenly, and then left the cubicle. For thirty seconds, the mother and I were alone. I caught her eye, understood the unspoken question, the buried anger, and felt the skin of my face heating up. I was empty, bereft of meaning, at sea. *Who is this God who would do such a thing?*

Eventually, I couldn't take any more and stood, feeling the skin on my neck still prickling hot as if burned. Passing back through the curtain, I faced a scattered group of nurses and attendants standing around a Mountie, a fellow named Gordie.

What did you say to them? asked Anne.

I shrugged, depressed and angry, like everyone else in the room. What the hell could I say?

Anne shook her head. I've been in this job a long time, she said to the group. Sometimes I think I've seen every kind of awful thing, but I usually let it pass, and sometimes I wonder if I'm just getting hard. Then something like this comes along and it shakes me. It's at least nice to know I can still be shaken.

I was on the scene, Gordie said. It was a mess. They had a little Ford, and the back end was smashed flat. They were still in the car when I arrived. They were screaming, because they knew the baby was dead. Hell, everybody knew it. I think that the mother would have picked that boulder up with her bare hands and thrown it into the river, but she couldn't get out of the car! They were pinned inside. I don't think I've ever heard screaming like that, but that's not what got me. No, it was seeing the boulder on top of the car. It hit them smash like a guided missile and hadn't bounced once. Like somebody heaved it at them on purpose.

When I was in the seminary, I went to a synagogue with an old friend. It was a tiny congregation that met in a rented room on the second floor of a used bookstore, and they were quite progressive. The room smelled of old paper and poetry, a smell that calmed me as soon as I breathed it in. The rabbi was a young woman who referred to herself as Liz. We sang hymns in Hebrew, and I tried to follow, like a soldier out of step, singing out the parts I knew and mouthing the rest. Now and then I coughed, pretending something was stuck in my throat. Then Liz chanted, prayed, read from the Torah, and we all sat down. She looked at us, her hands in front of her as if she wasn't quite sure what to do with them, and then said a word:

Yah-hah! She said, rising on her tiptoes, breathing the word.

The name of God, she said, should not be spoken. What is more, she said, the name of God cannot be spoken, for it is not a word, not a name like other names. It is a name that is not a name, a word that is not a word, a sound that is not a sound, but a name that is the passage of air out of the lungs, spirit, *spiritus, pneuma, kamikaze, divine wind.*

Yah-hah! The name of God is the name of nothing and of all things. It is breath moving in and moving out. It is the act of life itself.

If the name of God cannot be spoken, she said, then God is not someone who can be named, nor captured in a mesh of nouns and verbs, nor understood in a reasoned argument, nor revealed in a poetic insight. The name of God, like the light that we describe as both a particle and a wave, cannot be reconciled into a neat package. If you want to talk about God, she said, you have to get used to paradox, because paradox is the only rationality large enough to handle the question.

What a weak, sad thing words are, I told myself. Just because I can write a word onto a self-adhesive label and stick it onto an object doesn't mean that I know what the object is. Rock, tree, chicken, eagle, trout, Mom, Dad, Bowser, miserable baby brother. The names fluff up a comfortable illusion, a pretty madness that makes me think that each thing is familiar. I believe I know them, when I don't, and sooner or later, something comes along, something like the death of a baby, and shakes my world like a dog with a rat. For God is *that*. The Mystery. God is the One Who Is Always There, the One Who Is, and the One Who Was, and the One Who Will Be, and the One Who Can Never Be Known. Theology, if it is to have any value, must begin here and end here, like a spinning dog or a dragon swallowing its tail. All wisdom, if it is wisdom at all, begins with not knowing and ends with not knowing. That is, it begins and ends with silence.

I once heard of an old bishop in Texas, a man people called Big Frank because he was six-foot-five—*before* he put on his cowboy boots. He was, like most bishops, a regular guy, until the first pinpricks of senile dementia hit him, when he became famous. He went nearly blind, which meant he squinted at everyone, and half deaf, which meant that he shouted at everyone, and was stubborn, which meant that he ignored everyone. Even so, not having anyone else, they trotted him out two or three times a year to do confirmations and put on a show, which he did rather well. One time he stood in the middle of the nave of the cathedral, surrounded by a hundred seventh-graders all praying not to be called on, turned to one hapless boy in the fifth row, poked him in the chest with the bottom of his crosier, and said, "Hey, kid! What's the Trinity?"

The boy stood shaking and stammered out, "I don't know."

Big Frank turned away, walked a few paces up the aisle, and then turned back to the boy again. "You're right, kid! It's a Mystery."

Is that it? Is that the point? Is that life? Hey, kid! What's the Trinity? *Yah-hah! Kid!*

Mystery surrounds us. It permeates us like water. Somewhere in your life, the choice will become clear. You'll have a weary realization, a flash of insight, a gut sense that says you have gone as far as you can. You can either drive around in circles, or you can get out of the car and head off across the hills. You can make the choice, at that moment, right then; the choice to try something bold, something you have never done before. Life teeters on that moment, as if all the birds have suddenly hushed, waiting, and every face in the world is turned your way, wondering.

Two days after the baby died, I found a replacement for the parish and announced to the bishop that I was leaving on retreat. Frightened as I was, I would face that silence, one way or another. It was time to run toward it instead of away.

I retreated from the world at a horse-whipping, foam-flecked, saucer-eyed gallop, out into the mountains to see if I could find another way to live. I decided to set up my hermitage in a cabin I frequented on the shore of Little Shuswap Lake in British Columbia, part of a chain of lakes that runs for thirty-five miles up and down a butterfly of mountain valleys.

The road to the cabin starts wide and ends narrow. The Trans-Canada Highway worms between the mountain spurs, four lanes to two lanes and then back to four, swift and modern, until Chase appears from behind a stand of ponderosa pine, then past Chase, down the lake to Squilax and the turnoff, two lanes to one. The turnoff surprised me each time, and each time I jammed on the brakes and spun the wheel to the left, leaving the cars behind to fend for themselves. From there, the road was dirt, crossing the land bridge that divided the Little Shuswap from the Big Shuswap, onto an even smaller dirt road running back toward town on the other side of the water.

Along the way up, I stopped at Chase to fill my car at Ian's gas station. The town looked like a bunch of fishing shacks with faded paint, weathered wood siding, and steeply canted tin roofs. The center part was scattered along the eastward bend of the little lake, with the backs of white clapboard houses abutting the pebble shore. Now and then, a trout leaped, spreading circles in the water. Because it was late August, all the summer people had gone the other way, back to their lives, more tanned, less fat, with more sparkle in their eyes and well-being in their souls. That and a freezer full of fish. The town was suddenly empty, and since most of the stores catered to the summer people, shop after shop had begun closing for the winter. The few locals—a handful of loggers, their wives, some retired fish enthusiasts, a sprinkling of Shuswap, all wearing faded baseball caps—met on street corners to rejoice in the quiet and blink at the sudden emptiness of the place.

Ian had lived there only fifteen years, which meant he was a new arrival. He was a good secular fellow, a Mountie whose wife had left him years before; he'd been shot in the line of duty, retired, and bought a gas station in his favorite fishing town, then settled there into a case of world sorrow and a taste for Molson Ale. He had studied criminology in Houston, Texas, one year and returned with the hint of a drawl he never lost, so his speech was somewhere between Prince Edward Island and Good Ol' Boy. And though he talked a law-and-order line—he always knew who was wanted and who wasn't—he was there for everyone who needed him, and even for a few who didn't. I suspect that Ian may one day die and awake in heaven, more surprised than anyone.

He was rangy, with hangdog eyes and a weathered cowboy face set off by bristly eyebrows. Leaning on the pump, he recapped the gossip of the lake region:

Some boy near Salmon Arm got himself drowned. They were summer people from Saskatchewan. The mother thought a bear had taken him, but when they found him he was floating under one of the piers. I heard that the father stood on the beach and cried.

Woman I know with two kids has pancreatic cancer. Six months at best. Real shame.

Two smoke jumpers got burned to death on one of the big fires up north.

That damn firebug is still running loose, and no one knows where he'll strike next.

After that, the advice:

You'd better not stay out there too long, he said, leaning into the car window, the smell of beer heavy on his breath. That big fire's turned, so they say, and may be heading this way. Take care, eh?

Nodding vague agreement to Ian, I drove out of the garage and into the street, then stopped the car in the middle of the road. I had noticed it—a sea tang was in the air, an intimation of newness pushing itself eastward over the mountains, riding along on a warm front, heaving a cloud bank before it. I sniffed the wind like an old bear and searched the sky. Strings of cirrus clouds rode high on the new front, while behind a line of dirty gray cumulus obscured the sun. It didn't feel like rain, though—not humid enough. The clouds washed out the blue, leaving a gloom that would just sit on the world and do nothing, a gloom that would hunker there for days and days, irritating me and driving my spirit flat into the dirt. There was also a hint of smoke. At first, I thought this might have come from someone's leftover barbecue, but the curtain of smoke hanging eastward over the hills told me otherwise. The smoke had been hidden by trees until that moment as I sat in my car outside of Ian's garage. I moved to one side, and the cloud suddenly appeared through a cut in the hills. This new fire was a lot closer than I expected.

Once again, I worried about the wind. Rain we could handle, but it was a fire season, and a bad one. Wind without rain would make everything worse, whipping flames into firestorms, campfires into holocausts. I'd heard that the fire crews had been stretched thin that summer—young men and women from all over Canada had been climbing into the mountains in yellow shirts with Pulaskis slung over their shoulders, but it still wasn't enough. One after another, tanker planes flew overhead, belching fire retardant from their bellies. Now and then, fire engines raced along the highway. The red glow burned on, the smoke rising. It seemed that the whole world was on fire.

Past Squilax, the road to the cabin wound along the lakeshore, sometimes down by the water, sometimes farther back into the hills, so that the lake alternately appeared and disappeared as I drove by. I passed the Smiths' and the Johnsons' and the Owenses' cabins, and then drove past a stretch without any homes on it at all. I passed the Lucas family's cabin and then Dr. Bennett's cabin. His daughter was still out there, and she waved at me. The side road to my cabin had a sign buried in the grass—*sanctae fumae* it said, holy smokes—and beside that one big rock half obscured by the weeds. Turning down that road was an adventure. It dropped off steeply, leaving you hanging at the edge, where you could only see the lake in the distance, and the trees on either side, until the nose of the car suddenly dipped and you saw the path zigzagging down to the waterside. The cabin was on the left, hidden completely from the road, buried at the edge of a small cove, behind a copse of silver aspens.

Once free from the car, I carried my duffel inside, turned on the water and the propane, stood in the middle of the room and breathed, filling my body all the way down—chest, lungs, and gut. Hold the air inside for a count of two, an old Benedictine monk once taught me, and then slowly let it out, as silently as a cat walking.

It is amazing how much discipline it takes to breathe properly, breathing smoothly and silently, like curling barbells. Let your back be the superstructure, the old monk once told me, your stomach muscles the engines. Breathing in and breathing out, opening and tightening your gut as if you were singing opera. Inhaling and exhaling—neither one is more important than the other. Both are deliberate, mindful actions. On a Zen retreat years later, the director tried to teach me the lotus position, but I could never do it—I wasn't built for pretzel bending—so I always stood or sat in a chair or on the floor, Indian style. Breathe in and out, the retreat master said, like water flowing over a smooth stone. Have that image in your mind, he said, then let it go, until all you can think about is your breathing, and how smooth it is, and how silent. Count your breathing, and be aware that you are breathing. Say a mantra in your mind, a simple word or simple formula full of breathing sounds, and then slowly let the words disappear into the breath. Then everything you are becomes your breath, and your breath becomes everything you are.

When I could no longer hear my own breathing, silence dressed me like an old warm coat; I wrapped it around me and breathed again. The tension dribbled out of me, and bit by bit, I felt myself slipping away with each breath. A floating feeling seemed to lift me even as I stood there. Suddenly aware of the strangeness of it, my nose twitched, my face scrunched, my shoulders tightened. The cat yowled and scratched. Some atomic-sized alarm bell had gone off, and fear awakened and demanded to know what I was doing, because who knows where such silence could lead. The deep silence fell apart.

I left the cabin and went to stand by the lakeshore. The water lapped the pebbles, making a soft, loving sound like petting. A loon called, another answered, and my heart caught between beats. Could there still be beauty after a baby dies? I asked myself. Even now? *Who is this God?* I once thought I knew; I once thought I understood because I had a system of belief, catechisms and divine disputations, because I could read Latin and even a little Greek, because I had studied science and could read Einstein with the math left in.

Yah-hah! I said to the lake, and the air moved. I said it again, breathing in and out. Was this the name of God? *Eli, Eli, lama sabacthani!* My God, my God, why have you forsaken me? I said this name over and over, though it was impossible to put it into words. Was it blasphemy to try? Or was I not merely breathing? If this was the name of God, it was also the name of life, but what about death? What could it possibly have to do with life, let alone God?

Yah-hah! The first breath of a child, the first spirit breathing in and out. The last breath of an old man, sending spirit into the world. In between is all human life, breathing in and out the name of God.

Many individuals and small groups had come to the cabin to pray, scattering old religious pictures, pamphlets, rosaries, and magazines, the detritus of devotion. Piety seemed useless to me at that moment. Priests and ministers burn out faster than anyone, faster than doctors and teachers. They are surrounded every day by other people's pain, and either they grow a hard crust, withdrawing into themselves, or they take to the bottle, or they have crises of faith. I could never trust a priest who had not struggled through a crisis, because his faith couldn't be very deep. Faith is a muscle, a diaphragm for breathing, and needs to be worked.

I had had my first crisis three weeks after I was ordained. My second hit by the end of that year. I had one each year after that, and each year I would swear I was leaving, going off someplace to sell shoes or join the merchant marine. And then I'd drive to the cabin and slowly knit myself back together. Even so, piety had long since lost its flavor. It seemed like a pretty spectacle, a face paint hiding more than it revealed. Piety, it seemed, never reached deep enough into things. It's what most people think of when they hear the word "religion," a matter of believing more in a set of doctrines than in the Mystery those doctrines point to. Piety can be a front for a faith that has failed to mature. A mature faith devours Mystery, teeth chewing, tongue swallowing, and sips silence like old wine. Piety's answers, the same ones I'd been giving people for years, can seem like TV dinners in comparison. Bare piety dies when a four-week-old infant is crushed by a stone.

By late afternoon, I was thoroughly depressed. I slouched back to the cabin as evening fell and plumped onto the porch lounger. Someone had nailed a large picture of the Scared Heart to the wooden porch frame above the screen. A mild-eyed Jesus stared down at me, pointing to his heart wrapped in flame; I made a face at him and turned away. It's no wonder you have so few friends! Saint Teresa of Avila once said to God. The way you treat them!

All that evening, I sipped coffee and watched the water, the wind tearing holes in the clouds. At dusk, as the world turned blue, a single star winked into being. A sliver of moonlight danced a hootchie-kootchie on the water; the night whispered to me about a world unseen, above, below, beside the lake, in the calling loons and the shimmying moon. Now and then a tingle of wood smoke twitched my nose, and I thought of the fire burning on the mountains northward. I tried breathing exercises again, but they didn't work, because the harder I tried, the more desperate I became. A half hour later, I accepted the failure and decided to take the boat out. I chugged toward the middle of the lake, cut the engine, dropped anchor into the silent water, and waited. A fish splashed off the bow, a loon called off the stern. I felt small. The silence of the water possessed me, while the boat rocked softly. More and more stars appeared, until a faint ribbon of the Milky Way surfaced from the black across the sky just south of the zenith.

Silence thickened, and I fidgeted—nothing stood between me and my own feelings. In the years since I had become a priest, I had pressed my nose into all the terrible things you read in the paper—suicides, cancers, drownings, car crashes, all happening to people I knew, people I cared about—and each one like a nuclear flash had left an afterimage that blinded me to my old insights, and in my new ignorance I also became dumb. I came to the lake not to speak, then, but to listen—to the loons, to the wind, to the birds, and to the growing fear that maybe nothing made sense anyway.

The Little Shuswap Lake is roughly kidney shaped, like a really big swimming pool. It lies east-west so the sun rises over one end of the lake and sets over the other, and every morning I feel as if something cosmic is about to happen. Water flows in from the Big Lake through the Little River, a narrow connective about a mile and a half long, and flows out past Chase through the South Thompson River, which alternates between meanders and rapids all the way to Kamloops, where it empties into Kamloops Lake and pools there for a while before it picks up speed on its way to the Fraser, a roaring fast mountain river that, according to oral tradition, has swallowed entire airplanes, trains, cars, and buses. At the Little Shuswap Lake, the water is civilized, slow enough to spawn twisting fogs of mosquitoes. Thick forest comes down to the water on all sides, but is thickest at the northern end, opposite the highway. Populations of mule deer, elk, and bear—black and grizzly—hide in the bush, which is too thick for humans to move through easily without a chain saw. Sometimes a mule deer, driven mad by mosquitoes and black flies, crashes out from under the trees and splashes into the lake. Sometimes a moose stands stupidly in the middle of the road.

Daytime, the lake water is stirred by mountain thermals blowing up the river canyon and by any new front that happens through. In the evening, the winds die with the sun and the lake area hushes to the point that you wonder if there had ever been sound there. Now and then, a car honks at another car on the highway, or a coal train thrums up the grade and down the other side, but these are alien messages.

Summers, I spent as much time at the cabin as I could, running the boat up and down the shore, waving at the other hermits who lived along the water, running out my line, and praying for fish. In four or five places, wide creeks fed the lake, and salmon fry entered from the spawning grounds farther upstream. These are good places to catch lake trout because the trout queue up there to catch their limit of fry. On warm summer afternoons, I dropped anchor just off the mixing zone where the stream hits the lake and popped in a line.

Near one of my spots, an osprey mating pair built a nest on top of an abandoned telephone pole. The female sat on the eggs while the male was out scanning for trout. Every few hours, he flew back and dropped a fish in the nest, hopped around a few times, then flapped off for another. Ospreys are great collectors of things. The nest itself was huge—maybe five or six feet across—sitting on the telephone pole like a vast upside-down hat. John Steinbeck once found three shirts, a bath towel, an arrow, and his missing rake woven into an osprey nest outside his garden. Some people have found rope, barrel hoops, staves, whole fishnets, shoes, straw hats, rag dolls, tin cans, glass bottles, sponges, and even toy boats incorporated into nests. A friend of mine once found a rearview mirror. Nothing quite so exotic had been built into my neighbors' nest, though I once saw something that looked like a length of black electrician's tape hanging down. Maybe they were putting in a Jacuzzi.

In the middle of the lake, the sky opened about halfway, truncated on all sides by toothsome hills and jagged cliffs. The rockiest parts of the mountains were softened by thick growth, but in places the trees were smashed flat by rockslides, scars on the slopes. On rainy days, the mountaintops lassoed a cloud or two, splitting them, sending twisting streamers of mist down the cliffs until they evaporated in the warmth of descent. If you look over the side of your boat, you can see clouds reflected in deep water, gliding stately as if to music. Beneath the reflections, trout flash, dart, and disappear. Which is real, the reflection or the depth? You choose—the surface or the hidden things; the glint and ripple or the world that emerges dreamlike as a dark fish rising? The light dazzles, but the darkness draws you in, seductive, and you are caught wondering, gaping at it. Somewhere out there, hidden in the folds of the ordinary, holiness jangles the atoms; positrons and pi-mesons puff into and pinch out of existence. The answers to life are there, in that feeling, just out of reach, as much in the death of the baby as in the beauty of the night, in the suffering of the baby's mother as well as my own confusion. I decided to keep practicing in silence that feeling and awareness of life, because it was in silence that they had occurred to me that night.

Sometime around eight o'clock, I pulled my dog-eared copy of pre–Second World War German theologian Rudolf Otto's *The Idea of the Holy* out of my bag and hunched over it, holding a penlight in my teeth. I had read this book three times before, and each time it scared the bejesus out of me. I huddled into the cone of light and read page after page, feeling the vastness of the world. All my life, I had read about God, thought about God, spun systems of ideas about God, and made them sound good, but Otto shot them all down. God is more than reason, Otto said, and that for most of human history, God was not supposed to be reasonable, but a raw power, the terrifying power of the absolutely real, the numinous. An experience of God is the experience of a silent fire, an experience of utter destruction. The ego evaporates in the hot winds; the self reduces to a shadow on a wall left after a nuclear blast—or a comet, or a moonrise. I see my own life as a reflection on bright water, my whole world the surface of that water, where now and then the numinous, like a dark fish, rises.

The whole world seemed charged with power. *Mysterium tremendum et fascinans*—the mystery that terrifies and fascinates. Thunderstorms and hurricanes, waterspouts and tornadoes—the finger of God writing on the earth. *Mysterium tremendum et fascinans*—a sky full of stars, and each one a hundred thousand years away at the speed of light, black holes and quasars, dark empty space. *Mysterium tremendum et fascinans*—a universe made of particles and subparticles, virtual particles that shift in and out of being, paradox upon paradox, indeterminate, uncertain. The numinous is the uncanny, the strange, the wholly mysterious, the experience that cannot be put into words, the name that cannot be spoken, for it is no name at all, but merely breath.

At midnight, the round moon floated high above Salmon Arm, fluorescing the clouds, the distant mountains, and the white stretches of shore. There is nothing quite like fresh moonlight on open water. I sat in my boat, rocking a little and breathing. Under the moon, the water, the mountains, the forest, the sky shift personality, like a grandmother smiling over secret memories. On the shore near the cabin, something large broke the undergrowth, slowly, stopping now and then, moving on. Clouds sent stringers past it, glowing whitely. I'm like the moose in the road, staring. Words fail, reason fails, civilization fails. Yet I saw with the ancient Greeks: A god must live in this place.

Stretching out in the boat, I breathed in and out the name of God. Nineteenth-century German philosopher Ludwig Feuerbach said that we create our own gods, but isn't the opposite also true? Don't our gods create us? Not just as in the Big C for Creation, but also in daily life? Doesn't my belief make me the kind of man I am? If my god was a mean, nasty, Odin kind of guy, a god with tattoos, maybe an eye patch, and a bad attitude, would I not be a different man? Would I have been so broken up over the death of one child? I would not want to live in such an unfeeling universe, so my god must not be that kind of god. But innocents die every day and I don't feel every death. The problem of suffering has been raised by all religions. It is *the* problem. Buddhists claim that people suffer because of desire. Jews and Christians claim that people suffer because they desire the wrong things. So what about babies crushed to death by boulders? God is terribly silent on this question. God can be coy. When Job questioned God in the whirlwind about this, God's answer was something like "None of your business."

Nonetheless, suffering eats away at our assumption that God is good. Powerful? Yes, we can buy that. Omniscient? Maybe that, too. But powerful, omniscient, *and* good? That would be the best thing of all, but still I was haunted by that question, *Who is this God who would do such a thing?* Who is this God who with one hand makes the moonlight on a lake, yet with the other kills a baby with a large rock? In the face of suffering, we collapse into silence.

Like Job, I have spoken once but will not speak again. That night I slept in the boat, with the loons, who woke me just before dawn. As the sun rose and the birds breakfasted, I weighed anchor, chugged back to the cabin, tied up the boat, ate cornflakes, drank coffee, and tingled with the morning's promise and the night's mystery. Everywhere, sure and strange, life breathed the name of God, in and out, breathing, living, and dying.

Two

WHEN I WAS TWELVE years old, I joined the Boy Scouts of America and spent my first summer camp at Santa Catalina Island, forty miles off the coast of San Pedro, California, where the central rite of manhood was to circumnavigate the island in a war canoe. It astounds me today that no one drowned. Three canoes set out one summer day, the first of three days. Each canoe carried ten boys with a camp counselor, often not much more than a boy himself, as coxswain. We left Emerald Bay on a perfectly clean California day, bright sun and smooth water; the paddling was easy, the swells gently rocking the canoes, the counselors calling the stroke from the rear, and each of us digging in. With each stroke, we tried to re-create that perfect J pattern that they had taught us—the stab into the water, the stroke, the twist outward at the end. God, it was an adventure! The hot sun, the open ocean! To be tested, to push ourselves to the breaking point, and to come back smiling victory.

Emerald Bay was on the leeward side of the island. Off in the distance, we could see the hazy purple line of the coast, there where Los Angeles was, there where our mothers and fathers, sisters and brothers were living out their ordinary lives, swaddled in civilization. I remember thinking of them as I paddled, and thinking of all the other summers I had sat with my friends under the eucalyptus trees, trading baseball cards. By the end of the first hour, we were still paddling hard, on and on. About the third hour, a warmth settled into my muscles, comfortable but illusory, the promise of pain lurking close beneath. By the end of that morning, I had retreated into my own head, to other summers, paddling stroke after stroke into the sleepy blue fog of exertion mixed with memory. More hours slipped by, surreptitiously, like a burglar on tiptoes, while I paddled on. Four more hours and we reached the far northwestern tip of the island. As the sun set, the counselors turned us toward a narrow beach hidden between two rocky points, where we could camp for the night.

Get a good night's sleep guys, the head counselor said as we set up camp. Tomorrow, we swing around the tip and paddle down the seaward side of the island. Today was the easy part.

The easy part. I was exhausted, but unfortunately I was a boy, with the vitality of a boy, and so that night, instead of sleeping, I sat around the campfire with the other boys late into the night, wolfing hot dogs and beans—man food—telling scary stories, and singing raucous ditties.

Eventually, the counselors shooed us off to bed, so we curled into our sleeping bags and whispered apprehensively at every wild sound from beyond the firelight: Did you hear that? Somewhere in there, I think I slept a little. Once I awoke gasping in the dark. A full moon had risen and everything seemed silver and ghostly.

The next morning, the counselors toed us awake as the sun rose and we groaned to our feet. We were in a pissy mood, stiff and sore from sleeping on the ground, grumpy from lack of sleep. We packed the camp while the counselors made little speeches about camp etiquette, and in an hour, with our mouths still sticky from the peanut butter sandwiches we called breakfast, we carried the canoes into the water and paddled silently into the narrow bay.

After two hours, my muscles had warmed again to the paddling rhythm as we rounded the tip of the island, where we confronted the difference between leeward and windward. The swell had tripled in size and was coming in from the southwest, broadsiding us, so we angled into it and paddled as hard as we could to keep from capsizing. The wind picked up, waxing throughout the day. By noon we were paddling into chop, the bows of our canoes lifting out of the water. Howie was the first kid to ask the question that was on everyone's mind.

Are there any *sharks* out here?

By early afternoon, we were halfway down the top third of the island, a mile and a half from shore. In the distance, a hazy blue bay cut into the island—the Isthmus—our next camp. From where we were to the bay, there was no beach to speak of, only cliffs as steep as Dover, where the ocean crashed and grumbled and swirled. To the right was the open Pacific, with nothing but water—and sharks—between us and Japan.

There is always more sea, and I knew that in some unnamed part of myself I had come to see it. The Pacific seemed immense beyond proportion, a swelling, heaving mass of water without end. I felt diminished, and daunted, and yet elated at the same time, groping after a lust for immensity I knew was buried deep in the folds of my own terror, the way a pyromaniac feels watching a house burn. I paddled on in silence.

The world is too big for me, but how I desire it! Staring at a mountain pass or a sky full of stars, I am often afraid, and yet transported. It's a strangely erotic fear, like the prickly feeling you get in your crotch when you hang your toes off the edge of a cliff and look down. The world is all too much. A baby dies, and I am speechless. An osprey launches from a ponderosa pine, and I am equally silent. Silence sometimes comes from fear, and sometimes from wonder, and sometimes from both at once. The mother's face still haunted me, the exquisite agony, the startled wonder. I spent the next morning fidgeting on shore, trying to think of something I could have said or done. I replayed the events in my mind, then replayed them again and again. When tired of this, I sat and watched the sky. It was a blue summer morning, a day that grabbed me by the ear and made me watch. A cold front was pushing in, with jolly clouds on a wave of new air, white and roly-poly. As the sun rose, a touch of pink appeared here, a smear of mauve there, orange and crimson at the horizon, purple and blackish green under the trees. The birds stirred, splashed, and warbled; a trout leaped. A few minutes into sunrise, the first light slanting across the lake, I stood in the driveway next to my car, counting and naming the wildflowers in the hedgerows: Alpine laurel, trapper's tea, Canada milk vetch, Scotch broom, phantom orchid. I saw that each petal was soft with dew and morning sun, the sky reflected inside every bead of moisture. Each plant, flower and leaf, was *alive*, recapitulating in itself the immensity of all living things, spreading to the morning, blooming from out of its own charge of vegetable fire.

Ten o'clock. I needed to see more. It was all too much and not enough. So back to the lake. Coffee in hand, I took the boat out again.

I felt as if the day had thrown down a gauntlet, a challenge, a wager. The world was too wide. Could I find words big enough to hold it all? I took out my journal and wrote descriptions of things, trying to funnel it in. What color is the water exactly? That sky is not just blue; it is more than blue. The words reached and roamed. Sometimes one would hit—bang!—and I rejoiced. But most of the time, no matter how carefully etched the description, I could never get it all on paper. I felt everything, and everything was unspeakable.

At the heart of everything, of the spiritual life, is desire. The problem: not *that* you desire, but *what* you desire. The Buddhist desires freedom from samsara, from the endless wheel of life and death. Christians want God; that is, they want the one thing that satisfies all wants. Desire is not an evil thing; it's one of the noblest feelings we have. It is hardwired into us, in recognition of mortality, of finitude and incompleteness, essential to the true self that yearns for growth and spiritual perfection, the part that yearns for truth. What is evil is the desire for something not worthy of the true self. In a way, American consumerism, as bad a habit as thumb-sucking, is a twisted version of the true desire for the spiritual life, for God. Untwisting your desire requires a scrupulous honesty about what you want and how you go about getting it. First, you have to know whether the desire comes from you or from outside you. Advertising and social manipulation confuse spiritual longing with lust for ownership. Nothing I own could ever quench my desire, because ownership is too paltry a thing. Real desire is not about owning but about being owned, about belonging, connection, and love. Real desire is the bridge to the mystery, reality at its most profound, drawing me ever deeper. But separating your core desires from the cacophony of advertising is like picking out the harp in an orchestra full of horns.

I spend my life purifying my desire. When I am confused, I run this little dialogue through my head:

If I want chocolate, don't I want the best chocolate?

Of course.

If I want a car, don't I want the best car, a Jaguar or a Beemer?

Of course.

But like a gunfighter, the best always falls short. Sooner or later, a gunfighter meets his better, and sooner or later, the best thing in the world gets bested. There is always a higher rung on the ladder, and so nothing in this world could ever really satisfy me. No sensual delight, no sweetness of ownership, no glory of success, no perfect moment could compare with the overpowering joy you feel in the presence of the numinous. Your life project, therefore, your spiritual task, is to train your desire, to educate the palate of the heart. And it will take—and make—your whole life.

This is not a matter of denying yourself, but of opening yourself to the subtler, quieter tastes and textures of the world. Learn to see beyond immediate gratification; dig deeper than lust, and keep digging until you reach the soul's desire, burning like a hot coal. The deadly sins are baby things, immature desires, the vestiges of the things you wanted when you were a toddler and thought you were the center of the universe. If you ask, said Jesus to the Samaritan woman at the well, I will give you Living Water, and you will never be thirsty again.

The education of desire is the most profound choice you can make, because it is the decision to steal your attention from passing fancies and place it where it belongs, onto your heart's desire, the desire for that singular Good that fulfills without subverting freedom. For this reason, desire can sometimes be the most fearsome thing of all, for it calls for the greatest surrender. Fear and longing are twins from the same mother, for there is always desire in fear and fear in desire. You can feel this wherever you are, if you are open to it.

I wanted to be alone, so I went fishing again. For an hour or so, I nosed around the lake, looking for hidden coves.

The boat rocked softly in the ripples. I half-closed my eyes, watching the dance of sunlight lambent on the water. This is what meditation is, I thought—sitting in a boat, letting the world and the deep fish pass by. A trout jumped nearby, and then another. Stupid fish, I thought. They were feeding all around me, which meant that sooner or later, someone would buzz by and drop in a line, and then they would want to talk, mostly about nothing, or about fishing. I didn't want to talk about nothing, and I didn't want to talk about fishing, so I kept my head down and hoped no one would see me.

A motor buzz; I turned to see Dr. Bennett heading in my direction with a determined fishing look on his face. I sighed. I liked Dr. Bennett, but I was in no mood for his company. He was a big, friendly man, about forty-five, with a pudding face and saggy jowls. His wife looked much the same, and together they looked like a pair of bulldogs, lumpy and bewildered. (They had three daughters who were so beautiful it made me question the science of genetics.) He pulled alongside my boat, grinned at me, dropped in a line, and the two of us looked at each other. He was going to bring up the baby—I could see it in his eyes.

I will never understand fish, he said.

I blinked at him, wondering how to respond to this opening. Should you? I said to him after a pause.

Oh yes, he said. Fish need understanding.

I nodded sagely. And if you understood them, I said, then what would you do?

Why catch them and eat them, of course.

I don't think I understand fish, either, I said. In fact, I don't think I understand much of anything these days, so why should fish be any different?

Um, the doctor said. A long pause. We fished, eyes intent on the floaters.

Nurses told me what happened, he said finally.

I nodded.

Real shame that, he said.

I nodded.

Bugger all, he said.

I rubbed my eyes underneath my glasses. Doc, I said, I have a lot to figure out about that, and I don't really want to talk about it. Not just yet.

A slow smile spread on his face. You're right, he said. It's not good fishing talk. He looked at the water, and I looked at the water. The suspense thickened. Eventually, my skin itched and I reeled in the line.

Your spot, Doc, I said. I pulled my motor sputtering into life and moved on. He waved as I left, and the last I saw of him that day, he was sitting in his boat, still staring at the water.

I buzzed westward to the mouth of the Little River connecting the Little Shuswap Lake with the Big. A fly fisherman in waders worked the Little River, his line etching elegant "S" marks in the air. Presently, I powered down the motor and dropped anchor just to breathe and look around. A buck mule deer stepped onto the pebble beach behind the fisherman, lifted his nose and sniffed the wind, turned and disappeared back inside. In the air above the spot where the deer had disappeared, a cloud of mosquitoes vibrated with atomic energy. Then a fish emerged out of the deep near my boat, its back a sliver of ghostly silver, the rest of it hidden in darkness. My eye followed it until it was gone, and then I saw them, hundreds of fish squirming, wriggling, swirling, jiggling like virtual particles, popping in and out of existence. The universe was a tease, a wriggling mass of things coming and going, pop-pop, and all of us swimming in the deep water, wondering where the bottom was. Free from the limitations of human speech, the rest of the universe seemed wondrously, terribly fecund: silence pregnant with meaning, perhaps with God. *Who is this God?*

Flotsam from the Baltimore Catechism bobbed into my mind. The words floated up, cross-examining me in the voice of Sister Mary Francis, my sixth-grade teacher, who always gave me detentions.

Who made you?
God made me.
Why did God make you?
God made me to know, love, and serve Him in this world, and to be happy with Him in the next.

I reeled with uncertainty. I didn't know who this God was anymore. And if a strange God made me, I was a stranger to myself.

Years before, as a young Jesuit, I studied metaphysics with a man who thought that everything could be reduced to symbolic logic. Worse yet, everyone else in the class thought the same way. They were all math majors, which made me the only poet in the room, and I was cast adrift, floating on a sea of truth tables and conditional propositions. I didn't understand a thing, until one day in class, for no reason I could see, it all became perfectly clear to me—I was certain of it. Something was there, a mystic truth that called to me from the spaghetti of symbols they had communally etched on the board: the arrows, the vectors, the upside-down capital Es. Bravely rushing in, I barked out the first thing I had said all that semester.

I get it! I said. It's like this really big fish!

Time stopped. The teacher ceased writing a modal conditional on the board, his hand with the piece of chalk still hanging in the air. Slowly, the class turned away from the blackboard and looked at me, mouths open (like fish).

Nothing is *like* anything, the teacher said. It either is, or it isn't. That's it.

He turned back, finished his proposition, and then mumbled: Everything's *fish* with you anyway.

I have been confused, to one degree or another, ever since. Philosophy will do that to you, if you're not careful. In my world, thought begins with metaphors and similes. To say that my Aunt Marie is a tiger is saying something—something useful if you want to get to know my Aunt Marie. The nice thing about metaphors is that they are little packets of mystery. Aunt Marie is not a tiger, that's for certain, but in a surprisingly real way, Aunt Marie is like a tiger, even though the connection between the two is opaque. You see it; you say it is so. You can try to explain it, but it's like explaining the punch line of a bad joke: Don't you *see?* The monkey, the chicken, and the traveling salesman are all . . .

By that time, the joke is beside the point.

Because the connections in metaphors are opaque, they make a good language for talking about Mystery, and therefore about the world. The world, at all places and all times, is implicated with Mystery. The numinous doesn't just refer to God, but to everything. You see a mountain glowing amber in the evening sun. You see strings of mist hanging about an early morning lake. You see a single deer emerge from the forest. None of these need to exist; none of these are logical certainties—if *p*, then *q*. Mystery upon mystery. Confusion upon confusion. The more I explore things, the more mysteries I unearth. All my adult life, I have been a philosophical Rikki-tikki-tavi. Run and find out. What is this thing *like?* I say. And what is *that* thing like? I keep chasing after the metaphor. I have to find sense in words. I would never have admitted this to the teacher, but in that class I was as bad as the logic choppers and the truth tablers. I could not admit that I had built my house on a beach full of metaphoric sand and was merely waiting for the next storm to wash it all away. Oh, I could handle the bigger mysteries, the fact that there are three Persons in one God, the fact that Jesus was both Divine and Human, the fact that the Eucharist was the real presence of Christ, because they were abstract theological ideas, because they were "out there," and they hadn't caused anyone any pain since the fifth century. What I couldn't handle were the mysteries of everyday life. Where does a woman go in the last stages of Alzheimer's? She is sitting in the chair, staring at nothing, but where has *she* gone? Does love die when the beloved dies? Why do we have just enough time on this planet to learn to eat with a fork, tie our shoes, stand up on our own two feet, shout—What the *hell* is going on?—and then die? And that baby didn't even have that long.

But throwing the word "Mystery" around never helped, really. "Mystery," too, is just a word. I knew that babies die. Babies die all the time, but I'll never have an answer for it, not one that makes sense to me. That baby was just the proverbial straw on the camel's back. Babies die, and parents appeal to me with that ashen look that asks why and I have no answers. What we cannot speak about, says Wittgenstein, we must pass over in silence. Wittgenstein must have been a fisherman.

The afternoon slowly thickened into evening. I motored up to Scotch Creek, a string of cabins with two floodlights on tall poles lighting up parking lots at the resort. I switched off the engine and drifted up to the dock. I carried the gas can up to the little store, thanking God it was still open, filled the gas, bought a can of tuna, some cookies, a bag of marshmallows, a cigar for manliness, a roll of toilet paper, double-ply and quilted for extra softness, and a six-pack of ginger ale—cold rations tonight—some matches, and a waterproof tarp in case it rained. A night on the beach is good for the soul, I thought, and carried my bag back to the boat. Fishing boats buzzed shoreward; the lake quieted, emptied out, and grew still.

The sky deepened toward evening, the blue settling slowly into night as I entered the Little River, hoping I could get through it before it got too dark to keep from wrecking myself on the sandbars. I made the last turn into the Little Shuswap as the last bit of light faded, and counted the cabins along the north shore. The night was so dark I couldn't see the edges of my boat, and the only thing I had to navigate on was the string of porch lights marking the different cabins. I tried to keep as close to the middle of the lake as I could, to keep from snagging myself on a piece of log or banging myself into a rock shallows. Finally, I could just make out a narrow point of land, then the lights from Doc's cabin, and at last my own. Powering back, I let the boat coast in toward the floating dock, and suddenly, there it was. I tied up, pulled myself out of the boat, and because I was all alone and didn't have to look good in front of anyone, I kissed the dock. Twice.

Later that soft night, I sat on the beach by the small fire I'd made, soaking up the warmth and pulling on my cigar, thinking how much of life was just like this, sitting in the middle of a circle of light, with the great dark night just a dozen feet away. Desire, I realized, is as much a part of the dark as it is of the light. It is the knowledge that I am missing something. That lack is a part of who I am, yet it is not identifiable with who I am. So how do I know what I really desire, what will fill that lack? In my own life, I have learned to tell the difference between a Disneyland feeling and the real thing. This is the feeling you get when you meet your true love, when you do the right thing. It is the voice of truth inside you cheering you on, urging you to face life as it is, not as you want it to be. Disneyland is a great place for fantasy, but not very good for reality. The spiritual life is lived, in fact, in your laundry room, ironing; or at the bus stop when the kids come bouncing home. Embrace its knowing and its not knowing, its light and its dark, as you embrace your children. To grow, you must desire both the light and the dark, the knowing and the not knowing; you must love the drama of life, the poetry.

A year before, I had driven my car up the hillside south of Kamloops and watched as the sun set and the mountains all around slipped into darkness. The city lights came on gradually, and when the dark finally settled in, they made an amoebic shape in the center of the valley where the North and South Thompson Rivers met, stretching pseudopodia up both sides. Brave lights; brave town. That amoeba was what passed for civilization in our mountains; inside it people comforted each other with conversations, thinking they had a good bead on things. But anyone who drove to the top of the mountain could see how small, how precious was the light. The sense of the world must lie outside the world, Wittgenstein said, not to mention the inexpressible, which *shows* itself; it is the mystical. Philosophy and mysticism tug at each other throughout our lives. Philosophy and science are creatures of the light; mysticism is a creature of the dark. As a philosopher, I think that I can only know what is illuminated by reason; as a mystic, I think that I can know what is hidden in silence.

The next morning, just after sunrise, I drove to town to do some grocery shopping at the Chase Market—Groceries, Bait, Tackle, and Sundries—and waited until they opened. The Chase Market was one of the few stores that stayed open year-round. The outside was white clapboard with the paint peeling off, and there were patches missing from the roof. Inside, the canned goods were dusty with age, and now and then the milk soured before anyone bought it. The proprietor and his wife were plump, slow-moving people who always looked embarrassed about the sour milk but never did anything about it.

Back home, after I hauled my bags into the kitchen, I put the milk in the refrigerator and took a nap. I dreamed that I was standing in the middle of the forest, which was on fire all around me, mule deer leaping over burning undergrowth with terrible grace, catching fire and vanishing like leaves. Cars drove past on the dirt road, the people waving and smiling, while I stood in the high grass at the side of the road with my hands in my pockets, watching the blaze. Jackie Kennedy rode by in the back of a Lincoln Continental, smiling regally as she passed, and I thought "Jackie Kennedy?" and woke up to the smell of burnt toast. I heard someone moving about in the kitchen behind me, and turned to find Albert, the Shuswap schoolteacher from Dead Man's Creek, making toast for himself and preparing to fry a few eggs.

Nice kitchen, he said. Good thing you went shopping.

Did you wait until I bought groceries before you came over?

Naw. I saw you coming out of the Chase Market with bags, so I decided it was time I stopped by.

I nodded, wincing from the headache I had from sleeping crooked. My mouth tasted like kitty litter, so I staggered into the kitchen for another cup of coffee and a piece of Albert's toast.

Go ahead, he said. There's more where that came from.

I took my glasses off and pressed the heels of my hands into my eyes, then sipped my coffee.

Jesus, Albert said. You look like shit.

Thanks, I said.

You know what your problem is? he said.

No, what's my problem?

You're a white man.

I guess that's tough shit on me then, isn't it?

I guess so.

I nodded again, sipped my coffee and chewed my toast.

Worse yet, you think like a white man. You always want answers for things.

I think like a white man, do I, Mr. Berkeley, California, Mr. Marxist Revolutionary, Mr. Heideggerian Existentialist.

Hey! Albert said, hand on his heart. All us Indians are commies.

I made a face. You're the only commie I know on the Shuswap Reservation.

That's only because the rest of them haven't been enlightened like me.

Albert was the most educated man on the reservation, a fact that he fretted over constantly, because it was not just an education, it was a white man's education. He had been to Berkeley and shouted obscenities with the best of them, had studied art, literature, philosophy, theology, even business, and was expert in each of them, realizing finally that white people didn't have a clue about what they were talking about, and worst of all, they knew it. He was, according to his own mouth, one-third Shuswap, one-third Lakota, and one-third Scotch-Irish. It was the Scotch-Irish part of himself that he blamed for his bouts of melancholy, his rough temper, and his altogether nasty disposition.

We moved out to the porch, where we propped ourselves on loungers, each of us with a pile of half-burnt toast on his belly and a can of Coke at arm's reach. We sat propped up that way for a quarter of an hour, listening to the soft afternoon breeze in the pine, the occasional splash of fish in the water, and the crunch of toast.

There was this baby, I said.

Yours? he said. I paid him no mind.

At the hospital, I said. I told him the whole story after that—told him about the rock, the father, and the mother, the Mountie, the nurses, and the failure of words. All the while, I kept my eyes on the water, unwilling to watch Albert's reaction.

Bummer, he said.

I suppose, I said.

Another long silence settled between us. If I had been in Los Angeles talking to my friends, a silence like that would be taken for impotence and embarrassment. If people don't say anything in LA, it's because you've said something taboo, nasty, or incorrect, or you've raised an issue nobody wants to think about. You can feel people pulling away, staring at their shoes, trying to think up a way out. In Chase, though, on the Shuswap Reservation, long pauses were normal, and if they grew up spontaneously in a conversation, it was to let the words sink in, to think about them way back in the lizard brain, to baste in them, to let them decay into silence so that what you really think about them can eventually come out. Long pauses in Shuswap meant that people were listening.

I have a theory, Albert said.

About what happened?

No. About white people.

I grunted, sighed. Another theory about white people.

It's really a story.

Okay, so what's your story?

A long time ago, he said, everybody in the world was Indian. All over America, and down in South America, over in Asia, and even in

Europe. Everybody was Indian. There were no tribes, and everybody was the same, all nice and brown, with straight black hair and nice round faces. You're a white guy now, but long ago, your ancestors were kidnapped by aliens. They came and took all the European Indians off in big spaceships, and taught them stupid stuff. And that's how you got all white and pasty. And that's how you got those ugly blue eyes, and that's how you got all those stupid ideas.

Aliens.

Yes. Aliens.

So I shouldn't be depressed about the baby because I have blue eyes and my ancestors were aliens.

No, what happened to the baby stinks. Just stop asking so many stupid questions.

I pulled an Indian pause on him, letting this sink in, mulling it over at the back of my brain. I kept silence for another quarter of an hour, but the questions wouldn't go away, because they hurt too much.

It doesn't help, Albert, I said.

He shifted a bit on his lounge chair and grumbled. *White* man, he said.

I know, I said, and sighed.

Three

IT WAS A BRIGHT green May, and the sky was deep and unbroken, a smooth gradient of blue. It was the year I was ordained, and I was in the market for a bit of silence, so I had driven to the cabin for a three-day retreat. The next morning, I followed one of the feeder creeks back into the hills to see where the water first percolated out of the ground. I walked for seven miles, raising my arms now and then, dancing sideways through the thick underbrush. Here and there, the bush thinned out enough for me to see across the valley to the hill on the other side, where the trees grew wild and unruly. A high-pressure system had cycled in the night before, leaving the air fresh, clean, and still, and as I climbed, blades of sunlight angled through the trees, slicing through the ferns. Wisps of morning vapor floated through the beams, glowing amber, a thin line of fog hanging beadlike in between. An owl hooted invisibly from one of the trees nearby; the stream sang in intricate voices below, but there was no wind, and all sounds were muted.

Another mile upstream and I broke out of a thick stand of hemlock into a glade of quaking aspen that straddled the narrowing creek. The air inside the glade was humid, the glade itself silent and primal. Late-morning sunlight slanted golden through the trees, brightening irregular patches on the ground. In the middle of the glade, the stream poured over a two-foot drop, pooling at the bottom before it spilled down to the lake. A grouse whooped at me from the other side of the creek, while a whiskey jack called overhead. Entranced, I sat on a low boulder beside the stream and lit a cigar. Sitting there in the stillness, I felt I had stepped back fifty thousand years to a time that had never heard of automobiles or telephones, and human beings still ran as part of the forest. I closed my eyes and breathed in the silence. I held the stillness inside me as long as I could. Then something changed, a soft passage of air, a touch of premonition, a vibration in the ground, and I opened my eyes. A shadow approached from upstream on the other side of the creek. A four-hundred-pound grizzly emerged, passing easily through the forest, silent and huge. For something so large, so full of power, it stepped ghostlike, without leaving a wake in the brush. I felt like a diver watching a whale swimming past. The bear could have killed me before I had a chance to react, but it didn't look at me, didn't seem to notice me at all, only kept on through the glade to the cover of the trees beyond, on toward some unfathomable bear business.

I stood beside the stream, cigar smoke curling around my head, and gawked at the place where the bear had disappeared. The aspen glade had shifted, the ground had become holy. The hush had become a fecund void out of which anything could emerge, as if there was some natural orchestra waiting to play and the conductor's baton was poised on the downbeat. Was this the silence of creation, or the silence of endings; the silence of ignorance, or the hush of wonder? We stand in the world, watching for bears, gaping after mysteries come and gone. We think we understand, but then we find we know nothing at all.

If you sit in silence long enough, things will come to you. Whenever I am in a talking mood, I pursue the world like a hunter after prey. I plan, I set goals, I carry around a little calendar with a to-do list and a bandolier full of addresses. I jot down everything in a section called "day's events." Like a grizzly in the blueberries, I eat the world and search for more. When I am silent, however, the world comes to me, comes on its own, its very existence a wildness. Day after day, I sit openmouthed with amazement, stupefied with wonder. Silently, I no longer pursue the world, because like paparazzi, the world pursues me.

Naturalist Tom Brown, Jr., says that a good tracker knows how to sit still and let things come to him, which they will, if the tracker is quiet enough. And so the hunt goes on. Silence brings the world together, subject and object, no longer divided by an impassable abyss, but joined, as if someone has thrown a rope across the Grand Canyon and pulled the two halves shut. The glade, the space where the bear had been, the hemlock trees around me, they were no longer things to name, but things to sit with. Eventually, I gave up trying to grind them into words. I let them be, so that they could be what they are. Thomas Merton says that everything gives glory to God by being what it is—the flower flowers, the tree trees.

There was a point around two hundred thousand years ago that human beings learned to speak, to make sounds that said things. There was a time when I learned this myself. Now I have become so good that I have a hard time telling where I end and my words begin. Am I a biological machine for making words? Am I a gang of words that all got together and formed a mind? I think neither, actually; I think that I am not my words at all, that instead my words are my creatures, and I make them as God makes mountains. What I am is awareness. Just as a flower flowers and a tree trees, I awaken in silence. All the rest is invention. When I was a child, I learned to talk so that I could have an effect on the world, first on my mother, then on my family, then on all those other people who swirled in and out of my life. I still do this. As long as I can have an effect, I figure, then I must exist, and I will keep on existing. I come to think that I am what I say, and worse, that I am what people say about me. I get addicted to talk. Without it, I wonder, will I cease to be? But this is still an infant's way of thinking. When you turn to the spiritual life, you realize somewhere along the way that you are not your words, but something that is as mysterious, as ineffable as God. In fact, you realize that you and God share in the same Mystery.

This silence that leads to Mystery is an art form that has to be practiced to be mastered. I first learned it in the Jesuit novitiate when doing the Spiritual Exercises, this trek of retreat I made over thirty days under the tutelage of a guy named Phil. The point of this retreat, Phil said, was to listen to the movements of your own heart. What comes up comes up; your job is to listen. And then he sent me back to sit in my room, or walk the hillsides alone. Hour after hour, I sat beside the trail and waited for myself to come along, a hunter after ghost bears and magic shadows. Sooner or later, movements of the heart emerged from the forest, some full of joy, some not, and I had to pick through them like a gold miner sorting chunks of ore. When you are silent, things come to you, valuable things, and you have to know which lead to life and which to death.

Here is how to know:

1. Any movement that leads to God will create peace in the soul.
2. Any movement that leads away from God will create war in the soul.
3. Some movements may appear to be good at first, and if they are good, they will manifest themselves as peace. If they are not good, then the evil in them will manifest itself by wrenching things all out of proportion. Fasting is good, but starving yourself is bad.

Years later, I slipped away for a Zen retreat where the master talked about mindfulness, which he defined as doing what you do for its own sake, being present to each action, each movement of your body and your mind—being present to the dish, to the cup of water, to the steam rising from the tea. Zen, he said, doesn't end with sitting meditation. Meditation is only the beginning—the rest you do every moment of every day, drawing closer to the world in bits, until you are flat against it, cheek to jowl, in an endless embrace.

The night before Albert left, I lay on the lounger, my sleeping bag up to my chin, and watched the night. Albert snored from the bedroom. He had the kind of snore that sounded like an asthmatic bus with bad brakes, a sound that vibrated through my spine with miniature electric shocks until, without warning, it stopped midway through, a long snorting inhale and then nothing. I waited, counting time. Three minutes passed, and I thought he might have died, and I wondered how he could hold his breath that long, and I thought about checking on him, prodding him awake with my toe, or throwing cold water on him. But then he snored again.

Eventually, the night called me back. Loons warbled, a raven cawed. An elk whistled somewhere far away. Gradually, I swam in the silence. The moon had risen over the hills and shivered on the lake. It shone whitely through my slitted eyelids, the water disappeared, and I felt myself floating on air. Moonlight pooled on the sleeping bag, almost translucent—even awake, the night was impregnated with dreams, my inner and outer worlds mixing like river water flowing into the sea. Somewhere in there, without knowing, I fell asleep to the sound of loons.

The next morning, after Albert had gone, the silence returned. I spent the day with Abraham Heschel's *God in Search of Man,* and more silence for company. As day thickened into night, the silence thickened with it. The few birds that chattered in the trees gradually quieted—now and then a flutter of wings behind me; now and then a whoop from the other side of the lake. A bird fussed; a bird splashed—and then it was silent once again. Overhead, stars began to pop in. Soon the sky scintillated with them, in places lambent and alone, in places faintly joined into a silver foglike haze. Marking stars quieted me, and the silence flowed inside. I listened to see if the stars were humming, as I always expected them to.

Every year, the night sky swings around the same circle, and every year the stars return to the same spot. I suppose that over a million years or so, the spot will shift in the sky, but throughout my lifetime, anyway, nothing will change; the spot will remain fixed, and the stars will always return, comforting, orderly, grand as kings. The light I was seeing was a billion years old, some from stars that had blown themselves to dust millions of years before I was born. In that passage, places in the universe immeasurably far came close, as close as the back of my eyes. I leaned into the aluminum chair, resting my head on the hard back, and collected light. The lake at my feet had smoothed with the dying wind and now reflected stars, so the lake and the sky were an infinite mirror of each other. Somehow, God was there, I knew, though I could no longer feel it. I am one acquainted with the night, says Frost. I cannot account for myself. I cannot explain my own existence, or the existence of anything. Why is there anything at all?

The Koran says that Allah made the heavens in just two days, calling forth seven levels, each with its own purpose. God filled only the lowest level with stars. What fills the other six heavens, the Koran does not say. If something as wonderful as the stars fills only the lowest of the heavens, then what must the others be like! Is this what God is like? Is this what is at the center of things? I want to know. I need to know; but as the need grows, so does the fear. *Who is this God who would do such a thing?* For a second, I balance on the edge, pulled in both directions at once, lusting after wonder, and yearning for certainty. Instead, without much resolution, I sleep.

The sun was already up, bright in the trees, when I awoke the next morning. I shuffled into the kitchen and stared at the Mr. Coffee as the pot slowly filled, feeling vague, empty, free of desire. "So this is Nirvana," I said. Something moved outside near the porch, and I wondered if the bear had returned. Three weeks before, a mama black bear had led her cubs down to the lake and knocked over all the garbage cans on the road, then disappeared into the hills. No one had seen her since. A shadow passed across the corner of the porch, so I dragged on my pants, then slipped my tennis shoes over my bare feet, and, grabbing a cup of coffee, opened the door, checking both ways, then hobbled down the thin wooden stairs to the dirt clearing around the cabin. No bear. I peeked around the trash cans near the car, and then down at the lake. No bear; only Old Joe, Albert's Shuswap uncle, standing on the dock, his back to me. He was wearing a red-and-white flannel shirt, the same shirt he had worn every time I had seen him for the past three years. He was a bony man, the kind who ages by shrinking, sucking in all the thousand points of his flesh into one skeletal frame.

I walked down and stood next to him at the end of the dock; he was watching the water without expression, without giving any sign that he knew that I was there at all. For five minutes, I said nothing and he said nothing, and we watched the water. At the end of that time, Joe nodded as if in agreement with something he had heard but I hadn't.

Hey, Joe, I said.

He looked up at me, grinned a toothless grin, looked back at the water, and nodded again at the silent voice. He fingered the wooden rosary I had given him the year before, which he wore around his neck. I tried explaining to him that he wasn't supposed to wear it around his neck, but to put it in his pocket. Whenever I said this, though, he picked up the crucifix in his hand and showed it to me, as if I had never seen it before, and said, This is my Jesus.

Hey, Joe, I said to him again. Want some coffee?

He looked at me, grinned again, and pointed to the western end of the lake. That's where the big trout are, he said. They're getting hungry. They'll be rising early today.

I followed where his finger pointed. How do you know that? I said.

Off in the distance, I heard a soft *ploop,* and then the screech of an osprey. *He* knows, Joe said, watching the bird circling over the water. Then Joe looked at me, as if he had just noticed that it was me standing there. And I'll have some coffee, too, he said.

I expected Joe to follow me up the shore to the cabin, but he didn't, and so I had to fetch a cup of coffee and bring it down to him. Age has its privileges. Joe took the coffee from me and sipped it, then turned and pointed to a tall spruce near the road.

The eagles used to live in that tree, he said. But then all the people came, and they moved. I wasn't sure what year Joe was referring to, because I had never seen an eagle in any tree around the cabin before, and people had been living along this side of the lake for over twenty years. With Joe, however, the past was just the past, and the future was just the future; that simple, and there were no gradations in either of them.

I got to go into town, Joe said, after a moment. Albert said you'd take me.

Oh, he did, did he? I said. That was nice of him.

Yes, Joe said. Albert's a good boy.

I smiled at that, knowing the truth of it, but also seeing my revenge. For the next six months, I planned to remind Albert as often as I could that his Uncle Joe thought he was a good boy.

A half hour later, Joe and I climbed into my Honda, backed up the drive, and drove toward Chase. Joe watched the lake as we twisted around the shoreline and behind the hills, as we passed the old Chase mission church with its missing bell and its newly painted white walls, and into the town proper. He leaned toward me. I need some smokes, he said, as if this were a secret.

That's a nasty habit, Joe, I told him, and stopped the car across the street from the Chase Market. Joe had been smoking since he was a boy, and at his age, no one could tell him it was unhealthy. He grinned a naughty-boy grin back at me, climbed out of the car while I sat inside, and stopped at the side of the road. A car was coming, a late model Chevy, but it was halfway on the other side of town and was moving at no more than five miles an hour, plenty of time for Joe to scoot across, buy his smokes, and come back. Even so, Joe stood waiting, fingers in his pockets, while the car crept down the street toward us. I sighed, muttering, C'mon Joe, just go; but he waited, his face placid, until the car meandered past. A couple sat inside, talking and pointing at the buildings, obviously not paying attention to what they were doing. The car had California plates, and I muttered, *Tourists!* while the man pointed at Joe and mouthed, Look! An Indian! Joe stood in front of my car, his face unchanged, until they passed, and then he crossed over limping, his right leg a little stiff from standing.

The Chase Market had three picture windows across the front, so I could watch everyone standing around talking. The couple who owned the place was talking to a third man whose hands fluttered about as he talked. He must have said something funny because the wife guffawed, then turned away and hid her mouth behind her hand. The husband laughed out loud and slapped his knee. Meanwhile, Joe stood to one side, calmly waiting, his fingers in the pockets of his jeans. The third man turned, glanced at Joe, then turned back to his conversation. No one else acknowledged him or acted as if they had seen him at all. Meanwhile, Joe waited, tranquil. I was amazed. I had known the old man for three years, and most of the time, I thought he was just a little hard of hearing, but suddenly it was as if I was seeing him for the first time. Joe swam in silence, breathed it, ate it. His silence had wrapped him with a dignity that had soaked in, saturating his blood and intertwining with his DNA. He never complained—he had no need to; he was where he was and nowhere else. The world embraced him like a pair of well-worn jeans. Meanwhile, I was seething over how those people were treating him. If he'd been white, one of the summer people, they would have tended to him at once. The third man had begun another story, and the owner's wife was listening with a grin on her face. She tilted her head to look around the third man momentarily, the grin disappearing as she saw Joe, reappearing as she looked back at the third man again. In that one gesture, she had said it all, that Joe wasn't important enough for her to pull out of her conversation, and that she would tend to him when she was ready.

Damn, I muttered. Look at you. You should be ashamed of yourselves. You need a talking to. Play the prophet, I told myself. I had stepped out of my car and was halfway across the street when the wife noticed me through the window and smiled broadly, waving a happy wave. I was Father, after all. Forget the talking to, I thought. How about a forty-five minute sermon on hell and damnation? As I was crossing the street, I looked at Joe again. He hadn't moved and was calmly peering over my head to the lake beyond, a little smile on his face. And then I knew—the anger was mine, not his. Joe didn't need saving, merely patience. Sighing, I turned back to the car. Meanwhile, the wife must have noticed me watching Joe and must have connected us, realizing that I was waiting for him, because by the time I had gotten back to the car, she had excused herself, drawn a pack of Joe's brand—Craven A—from under the counter, and was handing it to him, taking his money, and shooing him out the door.

Joe walked around the front of the store to the street and stood. Another car was coming, an RV with a boat in tow, and it was moving just as slowly as the car from California. Joe stood by, still tranquil. I lowered my head to my chest, closed my eyes, and growled. Catching myself, I whispered—Patience, patience—and then in my mother's preachy voice—Patience is a virtue. Joe was still standing there when I looked up. He hadn't moved, and for all I knew, he hadn't blinked. The RV crept along, and I forced myself to surrender. I, too, waited, but without much grace. Drumming my fingers on my pants leg, I waited some more. That is the problem with waiting. You have to give up control of the future, and even of the present, broadcasting power to all the things and people around you, allowing their actions to dictate yours. And yet, that is what the spiritual life is largely about. All my life, I have waited for God, drumming my fingers on my pants leg while God steals the time. Anyone who wants to find God, a Jesuit from Zambia had once told me, had better find a nice street corner and hunker down until God comes by. Sort of like waiting for Joe, I thought.

The aim of waiting is detachment. It is the treasure in the field, the pearl of great price, the ultimate refinement of spirit, for detachment is freedom boiled into syrup. Freedom concentrated to its quintessence. Merton says that any attachment to a created thing, to anything less than God, is a disorder of the soul. Only the desire for God perfects the human heart, for only God is enough. Impatience is the offspring of the need to control. Detachment is freedom from impatience, freedom from desire for unworthy things. So the spiritual life, too, boils into syrup, boils into waiting. Waiting is an exquisite agony, and yet a release, a transcendence, an art to be tended. It is the marrow of the art of silence.

Eventually, the RV passed. Joe walked across the street, went around my car, and climbed in. He grinned at me, and then as we started down the road, stared out at the lake as if nothing had happened, nothing at all. I drove as fast through town as I legally or even illegally could, just to balance out the books, and at the Trans-Canada Highway turned west toward Kamloops, which was the "in town" in our area. As we drove, Joe watched the South Thompson River flash by, sometimes nodding his head at memories.

A bear lived up in those hills, he said, pointing to the other side of the river. A big bear. He killed my cousin, up on the creek that year. After that, we followed him up the creek to his place, and we hunted him. He made a very good rug.

I tried to get Joe to tell me more of the story, but he grinned at me and lapsed back into silence. The silence that he generated was like a force field, action at a distance, throwing my nervousness back into me, bottling me up. I wasn't sure whether it was wisdom or introversion that made Joe quiet. There was a cultural dimension to it, to be sure. The only really noisy Shuswap I'd met was Albert, and he'd spent too many years among white people. Joe was a simple man, but he understood things that I didn't. I doubted if he could put those things into words, but it really didn't matter if he could or not, because the things he had learned, he had learned in silence. Rudolf Otto wrote that silence is a natural response to the presence of the holy. I could imagine that, me standing hat in hand before God, afraid to speak, but Joe's silence was easier than that, as if he and God were brothers.

Watching Joe, I realized that solitude is the only way to notice what needs to be noticed, to see what needs to be seen. Joe processed nothing, gathered no data, arrived at no conclusions. I glanced at him as we drove, wondering if he had the answers I was looking for. For some reason, perhaps out of nervousness, I told him the whole story of the baby, of getting the call and hurrying to the hospital, and of walking into the alcove like Saint George armed to fight the dragon only to find myself powerless, weak, stupid, insipid, and foolish before the unbearable mystery of it all. I don't know what I expected from Joe, or how I expected him to help my weak faith, but the words came out anyway. At first, Joe stared out the window as I talked, but then he turned to me, his head slightly cocked, his eyes on me. He nodded, then pulled a cigarette out of his new pack of Craven As and pushed my cigarette lighter in. When it popped, he pulled it out glowing orange and set fire to the tip of his smoke. He put the cigarette lighter back in and looked at his feet while I talked on. I told him about Albert advising me not to ask so many stupid white man questions, and that what Albert said hadn't helped because the questions came anyway and that I felt that I was drowning in them and I didn't know what to do and I wasn't sure if I should go on and be a priest anymore or if God was good or if the world was good or if life was good and I didn't know what to think or what to feel or what to do about anything any more.

Suddenly running out of energy, I collapsed into myself like an imploding star. I feared that I had opened myself too far and suddenly felt depressed for having crossed my own boundaries. I waited for Joe to say something, anything to take the pressure off me, but he looked at me sidelong, fingered the crucifix on the end of his rosary, and then stared out the window.

That's a good place to fish, he said, pointing to a clear pool we passed.

I seethed the rest of the way into Kamloops. I was as mad at myself as I was at Joe. He could have said something, anything, an answer, *one simple goddam answer*, but then again, I shouldn't have said so much. I felt as if the air between us had been stained with foul breath. We drove down the long sloping hill into town, past the cathedral, where I was staying. At the center of town, near the bus station, I stopped the car and turned to Joe.

Where to, Joe? I said.

Joe pointed to the corner near the bus station. Right here is good, he said.

No no no, I said. Where do you need to go? I'll take you wherever you need to go.

He pointed to the corner again. Right here is good, he said.

Joe, I said. You came into town for some reason. Are you staying with your sister on the reservation? Where are you staying?

He pointed to the corner again, this time jabbing the air with his cigarette. Right here is good, he said.

I took a deep breath, let it out. All right, I said. Right here. When do you want me to pick you up?

Tomorrow, he said.

Where? I said.

Right here, he said.

Joe, this is a street corner. This isn't anyplace.

Right here, he said.

Okay! I said, my hands in the air. Right here.

Joe nodded, opened the door of the car.

What time? I said.

Joe looked at me, puzzled, then looked at his feet, his mouth folded, thinking. Tomorrow, he said.

Joe, I said. Tomorrow is a long time. Give me a time tomorrow, and I'll be here then.

Tomorrow, he said, and climbed out of the car.

Okay, I said. I'm going to pick a time, and be here tomorrow.

Joe stood, and turned away. Okay, he said.

Good-bye, Joe, I said. I'll see you tomorrow. Here.

Joe turned, nodded, and, after a moment's pause, leaned in the window. You're a good boy, he said to me, then turned back and walked up the street with his fingers in the pockets of his jeans.

Four

TOMORROW ARRIVED. I AWOKE at five to say the morning Mass, showered, shaved, and crept down the stairs to get coffee. Seven people attended Mass that day—five elderly Italian ladies who fingered their rosaries, the beads clattering against the backs of the pews as they moved; one young woman with a baby; and a businessman who sat in the back of the church, covering his face with his hands as he prayed. Now and then he scrubbed his face with his palms as if he would wash something away. Each person sat at a point equidistant from the others in the church, as if they were all part of the demonstration of a math puzzle. After Mass, I was in the sacristy putting things away when I overheard a conversation between one of the Italian ladies and the young woman with the baby. The young woman's husband was a tanker pilot fighting fires. The big fires are in the States, she said, and her Gordie is down there helping. As I left the sacristy, the Italian lady handed me a rosary to bless. The pilot's wife asked for prayers.

Walking back to the rectory, I thought about Joe standing on the street corner, waiting, his fingers in the pockets of his jeans. Most people sprint through your life, raising a cloud of dust. Now and then, however, someone haunts you, hangs around the white room in the back of your mind, for they have changed you, almost without notice. Joe was one of these. In outward appearance, he was just a strange old man, silent at his core, as if he had already completed himself. Joe lived in the present, nearly all the time.

Inside the rectory, Ma Mouncy, the housekeeper, stood at the stove, her back to me as she made pancakes and eggs. She mumbled something, then puffed on a cigarette. She always had two cigarettes burning simultaneously, one in the ashtray nearby, and the other dangling from her lip, while a curl of smoke forever floated over the top of her head. A slight woman, Ma cussed ferociously, suffered from labor-gnarled hands and a stoop in her shoulders. She had straight, brown-tinted hair, and every day she wore a puffy housedress and apron, with fuzzy slippers.

Ma had been working at the rectory for thirty-five years and had therefore become an institution, complaining every day about her back, her legs, her arthritis, and threatening to retire at any moment. She had been a destitute widow with two small children when the old bishop had found her working the berry fields, hired her, and built an apartment for her off the kitchen, where she lived for the next thirty-five years, watching the wrestling on TV while ironing vestments and raising her kids. Blueberry season started every year in August, and Ma knew she could make a stack of money quickly in the fields. So every August, she picked a fight with the bishop, quit her job, and then disappeared, her children in tow. One year, she told him he could stuff his new church up his ass brick by brick, sideways, and then with all the bearing of Queen Victoria, picked up her kit, which had already been packed, and led her children out into the world. Each year, the bishop quietly made do until berry season ended, and then drove to the fields, where he found her and rehired her, until the next August and the next blueberry season.

As I walked in, Ma pried two pancakes off the griddle and carried them to the serving plate. One of them slipped off the pancake turner, bounced off the counter, then flopped onto the floor. She froze, hand on hip, halfway between griddle and plate.

I could just swear, she said.

Go for it, Ma, I said. Startled, she turned to face me and gave me a squinty-eyed look.

You don't want me to swear, she said, cigarette bouncing up and down. Once I start swearing, I don't stop. I'm a bohunk, you know, and no one can swear like a bohunk. Then she stopped, looked at me, cigarette smoke curling over her head, pancake turner still in one hand. You'd better not go out to that cabin again today, she said.

Why not? I said.

That fire, she said. It's on the radio, and you know it's bad if it gets on the radio.

I looked out the window in the general direction of the cabin, fifty miles upriver. It'll be okay, I said, uncertain.

Ma motioned for me to sit at the kitchen table, then carried over a plate of pancakes and eggs, held the plate two inches above the table, and dropped it. Stupid, she muttered, half turning away.

How's that? I said.

She turned back to me, and enunciated roundly. You're stupid!

Well thanks, Ma, I said.

Ma turned, then shot back, You act like you killed that baby yourself.

I concentrated on my eggs, not wanting to fight with Ma. I was fairly certain I would lose. Luckily, she let it go, carried another plate to the table, and sat down across from me.

I hear you brought Joe Peters into town, she said.

I looked at her. How do you know these things?

She looked back at me, self-satisfied. It's a small town, she said.

Hunh, I said, going back to the eggs.

He used to be quite a rascal, that Joe, Ma said. Quite a ladies' man, too. Had a new girl every week, including Sundays.

You wouldn't know that from seeing him now.

That was when he was drinking. He was mean then, too. He was always beating somebody up. Finally, he beat up his brother Jimmy. But only when—

He beat up Jimmy? Why—?

Joe got drunk and Jimmy got drunk, so naturally they had to fight, and Joe was simply better at it. But when he found out he had put his brother in hospital, Joe got even drunker and stayed drunk for two months. He ended up walking down the middle of the highway, and a car hit him, shattered his hip. He was in hospital himself for six months, and when he got out, he was a changed man. Now he's all holy.

You think Joe is holy? I said.

Ma shrugged. I guess, she said. I don't know. Everybody says so. Everybody except Jimmy.

Was Joe holy? When I was a boy, holiness was for saints, people with pictures in prayer books and on stained-glass windows. Holy people were heroes. But then, I grew up and started reading theology. Thomas Merton said that holiness was having a relationship with God, and that all things that existed were holy simply because they existed.

What a sweet thought! To get up in the morning and be surrounded by saints and angels. To sit out in a boat and watch the stars and hear the singing of Seraphim and Cherubim. *Holy! Holy! Holy! Is the Lord God of Hosts.* If Joe is holy, it is because he is just Joe. To be holy, he doesn't have to be anything more, he only has to be unabashedly himself. But, I wonder, how easy is that to achieve? A yellow sunflower, a hemlock, a sockeye salmon, a pink carnation—all are holy.

While Ma and I were eating breakfast, Nora Cooper stepped into the kitchen and stood like the Queen waiting to address Parliament. Scattered thinly about British Columbia you will still find a transplanted remnant of the Empire—a little old man in a bowler hat, a lady in white gloves—making all the world England. A rear guard, they hold together the tatters of civilization. They serve tea at four, actually understand cricket, and declaim hockey to be barbaric. Every one of them endured the Blitz, or jumped out of an airplane on D-Day, or stood watch with the Home Guard. Everyone in England, it seems, had done something heroic in the war. Nora had been an air raid warden, and every time she described it, an image of her standing at the barricades, carrying a rifle, wearing a helmet with white gloves and a string of pearls, crept into my brain, and I grinned at her like an idiot. When the war ended, she'd emigrated to British Columbia, where she met her husband, Robin Cooper, at a barn dance. He had ridden a glider into France in the early hours of D-Day, and said that nothing in the war had been so unnerving as trying to fox-trot around the chickens that strutted underfoot in that barn. After they married, Robin took a job as the headmaster of the school in Chase, worked there for the next twenty-five years, and then died all too suddenly of a coronary. Nora spent the rest of her life mourning him.

Ma looked up and noticed Nora pausing at the door, but said nothing. Ma thought people should just come in and sit down, but Nora refused to put herself forward. Instead, she tarried at the entrance of the kitchen, her hands clutching a small white bag, while the two of them stared at each other. Eventually, Ma puffed in agitation and waved her to a chair. Nora sat, hands in her lap, and we began the formalities.

Good morning, Father, she said. I trust you are well?

Good morning, Nora, I said. And yes, your trust is well founded. I'm peachy keen. Nora smiled. She always made allowances for me, because I was from the States and had no culture to speak of, and one had to offer them a certain measure of understanding, if not outright forgiveness. I trust you are well also? I said to her, getting into the spirit of it and smiling back just as tolerantly.

Oh, yes, she said. Quite well, thank you.

Good-oh, I said, not quite sure whether that was English or Australian, and returned to my eggs. Nora then turned to Ma.

Good morning, Mrs. Mouncy, she said.

Ma puffed on her cigarette, and nodded. Good morning, yourself, she said.

A long pause followed, as we readjusted ourselves to polite conversation. Ma asked Nora if she wanted coffee, and she accepted, so Ma stood, poured a cup, and set it on the table. You take cream, don't you? she said.

Oh yes, thank you, Nora said, then poured a dollop, two, three, four, into the coffee. One teaspoon of sugar, then another. Stirred the mix, then laid the spoon carefully on the saucer. No spoon clinking for Nora.

Nora looked up at me then. I understand that you brought Joe Peters into town yesterday.

How do you people know this stuff? I said.

This is a small town, she said.

Hunh, I said.

How is Joseph, by the way? Robin and I knew him many years ago, when we first moved here from England. Robin thought the world of him, though Joseph was quite the drinker then.

He's fine, as far as I can tell. Ma was just telling me about his accident on the highway.

Oh yes, I remember that. He was hurt rather badly.

I looked at her, waiting for her to go on, and she took the signal.

That was in 1954, or 1955, one of those. That was the year the grizzly bear came into town and fell asleep in the nave of the Presbyterian church. It was in all the newspapers.

I nodded and forked up a mouthful of scrambled eggs.

Joseph's accident happened the year before the Elks Club burned to the ground. You remember the fire, don't you, Mrs. Mouncy?

You bet, Ma said. All that weeping and swearing and gnashing of teeth.

I looked at them in turn.

Some said Joe Peters set the fire, Ma said, and Nora shook her head.

I don't believe that, she said. It wasn't like him. But someone set it, or so Robin thought.

What happened? I said.

Nora leaned forward, as if to pass along a confidence. The Elks Club was the only licensed tavern in the area, she said, and it was an evil place. There were fights almost every night, and loud music—that country and western music they'd imported from the States. Nora stopped and looked at me as if it was my fault. Women of bad reputation worked there, too, she said. The place was a den of sin, and Robin and I enjoyed it very much. Not that we ever visited. We didn't have television up here at the time, and so listening to the riot was our chief source of entertainment. In the summer, we sat out on our veranda with a glass of sherry, argued about Chaucer, and listened to the goings-on. Women screamed, then laughed; men shouted; there was glass breaking, while Robin and I speculated about who had pulled a knife on whom, and what logger was sleeping with what miner's girlfriend. Sometimes in the winter, we could see the heat pouring out of the windows like steam. Every Saturday night, someone tottered out the front door and threw up on the steps. All the ministers in town preached against it, but nothing changed. Until it burned to the ground.

Burned right to the ground, Ma said, nodding.

What does Joe have to do with this? I said.

Well, Nora said and looked prim. The year before, he had had his accident, and while he was still in hospital, he had sworn off liquor entirely. He had worked through five of the twelve steps, but the Elks Club was still there, a sore temptation.

You think Joe started the fire? I said.

No, Nora said.

Yes, Ma said.

No one knows, Nora said. And no one knows how it started, either. Some say it was a grease fire, some say it was electrical, some say it was set intentionally. Personally, I accept the last theory. I think it was someone who worked there, someone with a grievance, but I won't say who. Nora looked smug, as if she really knew. Joseph was newly sober at the time, she said, and Robin told me he struggled constantly against his former life but was losing. As things were, he would probably have gone back to drink, but then the fire started.

I still don't see what Joe has to do with any of this.

Ma waved me to silence. Hold your water, she said.

The night of the fire, Robin and I were standing on the veranda, as was our custom. We didn't know anything about the fire until someone started shouting, The Elks Club! The Elks Club! It's on fire!

I can't imagine the Elks running a wild bar, I said. Sounds funny. The Knights of Columbus I could see.

After that first cry, we heard wails, Nora said. Shouts of despair. We saw the flames then, curling over the roof of the building, and smelled the smoke. The clubhouse was an antique clapboard building with a tin roof, and Robin said that the floorboards were so saturated with cheap liquor they were on the brink of spontaneous combustion. Within fifteen minutes, the fire consumed the building. Luckily, the club sat far enough away from other buildings, and there was no wind that night, or the whole town might have gone with it.

Close call, I said, thinking of the forest fire near the cabin.

People, mostly young men, stood around in herds, hands in their pockets, shaking their heads as if war had been declared. One poor fellow fell to his knees, his arms outstretched like an ancient prophet. It was all quite biblical—

End of the world stuff, eh? I said.

Apocalyptic. Robin, who was always ready with a quote, opened up a bottle of brandy we had been saving for just such an occasion, produced two snifters from the kitchen, and the two of us toasted the Elks Club from our veranda. Fallen! Fallen! Fallen is Babylon the Great, he said, and raised his glass. My phonograph collection included an old copy of "Nearer My God to Thee," but I couldn't find it. Pity.

And Joe? I said.

I was just coming to that. As I was stepping out onto the veranda from the bedroom to complain to Robin that he really should put the phonograph records back in order, I saw Joe standing across the street, fingers in the pockets of his dungarees and a look of angelic peace on his face.

See? I told you, Ma said. I told you he set the fire.

No, no, Mrs. Mouncy, you don't understand at all, Nora said. Everyone in town was either weeping or celebrating, but Joe did neither, only stood silently by, as if he had just been released from prison.

See? Ma said. That's proof. He started it.

You just want to be dramatic, Ma, I said. I don't think he did it.

Ma snorted and puffed on her cigarette. Why not? she said.

I shrugged. I don't know. I just don't think so.

Ha! Ma said. I think he set that fire. On purpose. I would have.

After that, the conversation turned to the Wrestling, Ma's favorite topic. Nora sat politely listening to an account of Count Viperon's defeat at the hands of Blue Boy, and how the Count had demanded a rematch because, well, he'd been cheated. I excused myself and strolled by my office to check the mail and grab a few more books. My thoughts turned back to Joe. Could he have set that fire? Possibly. Something had happened that night, something that had changed him, freed him, stripped him down to the bare truth. The Joe I knew was indifferent to his own comfort, to desire for power, for luxury, for ownership. Saint Anthony of Egypt walked out on his comfortable middle-class home in Alexandria to survive among the tombs, and there he nightly wrestled with demons. Saint Francis of Assisi, after returning from war, stripped the finery from his back, dropped them at his father's feet, and walked out of the town naked. The prophet Elijah, after beheading the prophets of Baal, wandered into the desert, sighing that he was no better than his fathers. Soon after God came to him as a tiny whispering sound. Such people were holy. Or perhaps mad. So where does madness end and holiness begin? An image of Joe as an Old Testament prophet setting fire to the Elks Club flittered through my mind, and I shook it off.

An hour later, I arrived at the corner, hoping to find Joe. I wasn't quite sure what I would do if he wasn't there. A wheat train had frustrated me on the way over; I had been forced to sit in my Honda and watch one squealing train car after another pass by. My only entertainment was the three little girls who stood on the corner next to the railroad signal. Two counted each car, their forefingers beating the air with each passing car, while the third girl did a little wiggle dance off to one side. One hundred forty-seven cars was my count, and I vaguely wondered if they got the same. None of them seemed bored waiting for the train to pass. Maybe the wiggle dance helped.

Down the street past the train, Joe stood at the corner, fingers in his pockets as I drove up. I was puffing and anxious over the train when I arrived, fretting about Joe standing there for hours, admonishing myself to be more punctual next time.

Hope you didn't wait too long, Joe, I said. I got caught behind a train.

Joe looked at me, puzzled, as if I had just said something in Swahili. Then he grinned and was silent.

How was your day, yesterday? Do anything fun?

Joe shrugged.

Visit family? Go to the store? I knew I was prying, but told myself I was doing it out of concern for the old man.

Joe shrugged.

So what did you do? I said.

I was up at the Royal Inland, he said.

At the hospital?

Joe shrugged, then nodded. I got something in my brain, he said.

What? A tumor or something?

No. Something else.

Does it have a name?

Joe grinned and shrugged. Albert had told me a few months before that Joe had suffered some paralysis in his right hand, but hadn't told me anything else. Joe was an old man, and old men get sick, Albert had said, as if it meant nothing, but I knew the thought of losing Joe shattered him.

Conversation ended after that. As we drove into the open country, I watched Joe sitting silently, fingering the crucifix of the rosary he wore around his neck. Abbot Moses of Scete once told a brother who came to him for advice to go sit in his cell, and his cell would teach him everything. Perhaps silence itself is the teacher. I had been looking for answers in theological formulas and had failed. Joe had found another wisdom, maybe a Shuswap wisdom.

As we drove, Joe watched the mountains and the fields. I expected him to be agitated, or even mildly nervous, with "something in his brain," but he was calm, as if he were listening to music. There was an air of expectation about him. Somehow I felt a fellowship of silence between us. The intimacy was in the silence; it germinated inside it, took root and flowered. I felt as if I had been running a marathon, a race started so long ago that I had forgotten its beginning, tracing out the same circle on the same track, over and over, always coming back to the same point, always thinking the same thoughts, and always feeling the same feelings. But when I was with Joe, I felt as if someone had said "rest," and I could stop, bend over, palms on my knees, and swallow air.

We watched the thundercloud of black smoke from the distant fire pouring into the sky, curling, billowing, caught in the winds aloft, the smoke pulling eastward, stretching out at the top, as if some giant had stuck its head into the clouds and had its hair caught in the wind.

You want off here in town?

Joe shook his head. Albert will be down there, he said.

At the cabin?

Joe nodded.

I grunted. Albert probably jimmied the lock, I said.

The wind was picking up. Maybe there would be more clouds, and hopefully a bit of rain. I fussed over this all the way down to the cabin, wondering if I should pack my bags and head to town. The fire was moving. In just one day, it had grown into a serious threat.

I found the little rock, the patch of weeds, the road that disappeared, and turned into it. Albert was standing in the road near the steps to the cabin door.

How are you and Joe going to get out of here?

Well, Albert said, and looked over his shoulder at the wall of smoke rising over the trees. We could turn ourselves into birds and fly to town.

You could do that, I said.

But that's only if it gets bad. Albert bent down and looked past me to Joe on the other side of the car. Hey, old man, he said.

Joe grinned. Hey, kid, he said.

How's he doing? Albert said to me, as if Joe suddenly stopped being there. Because Joe was old, he could quickly become invisible.

He's got something in his brain. I don't know what. Joe doesn't know what, either, do you Joe?

Joe shook his head. Nope, he said.

You die on me, old man, and I'll be pissed as hell, Albert said.

Okay, Joe said.

Hunh, Albert said, and straightened up. I don't know what we're going to do about this fire.

Is the town threatened?

No, but you never know.

I think I'll probably stay for a while.

Albert looked at me. Well, if you're going to stay, then I'm going to stay.

I don't know what I'm going to do. Should we get Joe out of here?

The old man will be all right. He's been through fires before.

Well, if we need to get him out, we should do it soon.

He ain't going to go.

Why not?

This is his home. He's a stubborn old man.

Look, Albert. We should all get him out of here, sooner or later.

Would you come back out afterward?

Maybe.

Albert looked up at the column of smoke. You're as stubborn as the old man. You don't think I'm going to let a white man come back and help save our forests while a true red-blooded Shuswap Indian, native to these shores, stays behind in town, do you?

Probably not, I said.

Albert and I spent the rest of the afternoon talking about the fire, making plans and counterplans, and talking about Old Joe's health. The three of us ate out on the porch—ham sandwiches and smoked salmon with slightly cooled Cokes. After lunch, Albert and I talked on while Joe moved out to the shoreline to sit on a fallen log and watch the lake. As afternoon bent toward evening, Albert went out to check on the old man. I found the two of them standing on the pier. They were staring northeast at the hills on fire. A red glow had pushed into the sky, and now and then a lick of flame crested the hill. Helicopters carrying buckets on cables flew into and out of the hot zone, dropping red chemicals that seemed to be simply swallowed by the fire, with no effect. I could almost feel the heat of it. Albert and I looked at each other, and I saw the gears working in his head.

Big mother fire, I said.

Joe gave me a tiny shake of his head and looked back at the fire.

I itched to say something profound, something foreboding and apocalyptic, but nothing I could say would help, so I held my tongue.

The fire burned on, a holocaust of wildlands, a sacrifice of timber and animal flesh, of habitats and soft waterfalls. Joe smiled at me and turned to look out over the lake, his fingers tucked into the pockets of his jeans. His smile passed from me to the lake, and to the fish in the water, and to the birds overhead, to the clouds and to the sky. Watching him, I teetered again on the edge of speech; but then, with a deep breath, I let all things pass into silence.

II
The Second Circle of Silence
NO THOUGHT

I know this happiness
Is provisional:

the looming presences—
great suffering, great fear—

withdraw only
into peripheral vision:

but ineluctable this shimmering
of wind in the blue leaves:

this flood of stillness
widening the lake of sky:

this need to dance,
this need to kneel:

this mystery:

DENISE LEVERTOV

Five

STANDING ON THAT PIER, still gaping at that fire, I was glad at heart that I had finally learned my lesson. From now on, I would dedicate my life to the art of silence, hand over the heart, swear to God, hope to die, Boy Scout's honor. Let all things pass into silence, I told myself. Let it all pass. At that, my brain started spinning like an overheated engine. One thought vaulted over another, contorted into memories, drawing in dreams, terrors, patches of paranoia, gyrations of lust. I was spun into half-remembered conversations, bent into forgotten irritations, a jittery mass of old embarrassments and a catalog of stupid things I wish I had never said. My brain chattered like three dozen five-year-olds at the zoo.

When Albert and Joe wanted to leave I thought, Good God won't it be sweet to finally be alone, but then I felt depressed because I wasn't sure I wanted to be alone, so I offered to chauffeur them into town to buy Joe's smokes and to drop Albert off at the garage so he could pick up his car. When I returned to the cabin, I told myself I was relieved to be alone, finally, even if the place felt empty, and even if I felt strung out, so I played fifteen hands of solitaire, cheated outrageously, listened to the radio for 2.3 minutes, and then stood at the kitchen sink to do the dishes, but couldn't bear the thought of it, so I quit. What's wrong with you? I thought. This is it, this is *it*, what you wanted, to be alone, to not think, to not answer other people's questions, and to not chew on every little worry or rub at every little problem until it becomes a sore in your mouth. And surely this is the life, I told myself, just staring out the window silently. So why am I bitching? I snagged a book on Zen and stretched out on the porch. Within an hour I had finished that book and was mulling over reading another book on Zen, but that seemed excessive, and not really very Zen-like. I opened the second book anyway, and read how Zen master Joshu told a monk to wash his dishes, and the monk saw the truth therein.

I stared at the page—shit. I've got to do the dishes anyway. Taking the hint, I grumped back into the kitchen and looked for the soap but couldn't find it. I searched for the scrubbing pad and couldn't find it. Then I glanced under the sink and found the soap but no scrubbing pad, so I washed the dishes with my hands, scratching at the dried-on pieces of egg with my finger, and rubbing the grease spots with my thumb. Should I become a Buddhist? I thought. Why not? No, no, I would become a monk, an anchorite, a stylite, a holy man, a nonsectarian holy man, alone in the desert, or in the mountains, whatever, and I would grow a long white beard, and inhabit some abandoned cabin, and swell in wisdom, and raise Swiss chard and new potatoes, and read Thoreau, and never open my mouth again. Beans, too. I would raise beans.

My brain was both running fast and frozen solid at the same time, like a hundred-car pileup at rush hour. Inside my head was the crashing of metal and the honking of horns. People stood beside their cars and shouted, shook their fists, fanned themselves, and lit one cigarette after another. Monkey mind! That's what the Buddhists call it. Monkey mind! It's when your brain swings from tree to tree, hand over hand, branch to branch, tumbling, jitterbugging, then dropping, never stopping, nervous, flittery, twitchy, monkey dancing from hope to fear to dream to lust, out of control, out of control.

You thought you were in charge of your own brain. You thought this because you had not been listening hard enough. Spend some time in silence, try to focus on one simple thing, a word, a phrase, for just a few minutes, and watch how your brain slips aside, a slick eel, and wriggles on to other ideas. If you tune in to your brain noise, you will find that most of the time your thoughts run on automatic: God, I wish I could lose ten pounds my nose is too big that guy cut me off I wonder why she's looking at me like that God that's an ugly dress I wish I could lose ten pounds I could sure go for a bagel right now got to send a note to Dad I wonder if he liked the gift I gave him these shoes pinch my clothes feel too tight I've got to give up smoking I sure hope we get that contract God I wish I could lose ten pounds. You will hear obsessions, fears, resentments, lusts you never thought you had, and will embarrass yourself to death. And the obsessions will coil upon themselves, and you will find yourself thinking the same thoughts again and again. And you will replay old memories you thought you had long forgotten, nurse old wounds, rub old angers, tickle old grievances. Nothing is ever forgotten, and sooner or later everything bubbles up in the stew. It's a miracle we act rationally at all.

In my third year of college, I developed a sudden and unexplained addiction to the writings of William James. He seemed chatty, the kind of guy I could hang with and talk philosophy over a pizza and a pitcher of beer. That was my favorite thing to do in college—get snockered over dead philosophers. My favorite James essay was "The Sentiment of Rationality," in which he treated reason as a feeling rather than as a set of rules. James thought that the marks of rationality were "a strong feeling of ease, peace, rest," and that "the transition from a state of puzzle and perplexity to rational comprehension is full of lively relief and pleasure." Somewhere into the third pitcher, I explained to my friends that the advent of rationality was like a sneeze. There you are, your sinuses blocked, your nose itching, your mouth twitching, your face contorted, your hand in the air to tell everyone to leave you alone until the denouement. You climb up, up, up, then over the top like a roller coaster, and then you sneeze! Everything opens. Everything is free and clear, and you go Ah! The same is true, I explained, of rationality. Your mind is blocked, thwarted, hindered, and you feel stuck. The frustration level rises, the itch to understand mounts, then you take a walk or sit alone on a train and the gears shift. The log jam breaks and you understand, and you go Ah! And this, I told them, jumping monkeylike into Buddhism, is the sudden cessation of monkey mind. Reason, I told them, is not so much a set of rules but peace of mind, the soothing of the shivaree, a quick freedom from the clutter. In that state of rest, I said, the mind sees clearly.

My friends all said, Yeah man! Way cool! and poured me another glass of beer.

Oh I could talk it, especially after four mugs of beer, but could I do it? Everything itches when I stop talking. All my chatty outsides get thrown into my chatty insides and I feel snarled. Like someone who has just quit smoking, I don't know what to do with my hands. I sit in the chair. I get up and get a beer. I come back. My brain races, and my thoughts jumble, and I only want to escape from that awful, quiet place. So what will save me from my own monkey mind?

It's not that I don't know the answer. I do. I just hate it. If the answer were to run away, to hide, I would do so gladly; but it isn't, and I know it. I have this meditation retreat master inside my brain, like an artificial intelligence programmed from years of spiritual books and long hours on my knees, and he tells me the truth whether I want it or not. He's a short, fat, bald Jesuit who smokes stogies, has a red Irish face and a voice like an old gravel highway. I think he was once a marine. He says to me: You have to keep going, kid. You can't be a quitter. Only sissies are quitters. I say to him: Who are you, Knute Rockne? He says to me: Look kid, this is just like learning the piano. You feel awkward at first and your fingers go where they want, but it all works out in the end. You just have to keep at it. It's easy once you get started. I say to him: Oh no! This is much worse than playing the piano. At least I have the piano to pound on, but in silence I sit there with all those damn feelings rolling around inside me like bowling balls. He says to me: That's nothing! Keep going, and don't be a weenie. He puffs on his cigar. You'll get control of those feelings eventually. Don't give up. Never give up. Put your head down like an old mule and keep going. I say to him: Oh sure, that's easy for you to say. You're just a figment of my imagination. I'm the one out here suffering. I have nothing to do! At least give me a book to read. He says to me: Chickenshit, kid! Silence is easy when you have a book to read. It's sweet as pie to sit in a big fluffy chair with a book in hand, iced tea in the summer, hot chocolate in the winter, but why not bring along your TV? That's not practicing silence and you know it. Silence only starts when you leave all your intellectual fun over *there*, on the shelf to be pawed at some other time. Contemplation takes guts. You've got to put everything aside and then see what boils up from inside. Sooner or later, you'll find peace. I could give you ten thousand techniques, but if you don't persevere, if you don't keep going, none of them matter worth spit. Never give up, kid, he said, poking at me with his cigar.

The next morning before the coffee kicked in, I felt a peace, a grumbly, stupid, brain-dead peace. I stared at the coffeepot, as I usually do. Somewhere inside my brain, I realized in a vague way that this was not meditation, but just another form of monkey mind. My brain, sans caffeine, didn't have enough raw energy to shout, and so it grumbled. Prayers, notations of interest, nonsense words, and obscenities all flowed out with equal force. Monkey mind is not consciousness but unconsciousness. The sea of dreams that floats the waking world. When I sleep, the cacophony of voices metamorphoses into a cacophony of worlds. The beautiful woman, the toaster, the flock of birds, the clock and the half-spoken conversation that seems pregnant with meaning transmogrify one into the other, in strange juxtapositions.

I will be silent, I tell myself, for a time, for *this* time. I will sit here in the middle of this room, without noise, without stimulation, without a past or a future, without a schedule or a to-do list or a single appointment. Those distractions will still exist over there, in that other life, for right now, for this moment. I will go back to them soon, but not now. That is the choice. It will seem perfectly simple, rational, restful even for the first thirty-five seconds. The hard part comes after that.

I will pick a room, any room. Close the drapes and the venetian blinds. Shut out the world as best I can. Light a candle. Breathe. The first thing to face is the fear: fear of change, fear of difference, fear of losing everything I have yet become. Most of this is scare-myself fantasy, but it is there even so, because I've brought it into the room with me. Who am I really? Do I want to know? What will happen to me? Is this madness? What will the neighbors say? God help me, am I turning into some New Age freak? I let these thoughts go, let them pass, let the fear flow over my head. Make the choice. Breathe.

For me, although certainly not for everyone, real meditation is something that can only happen after coffee, after I have been sitting awhile, or have walked a few laps zombielike around the yard. I have to have enough time to allow the shards of my identity—where I am, who I am, what I am doing here—to gather themselves and begin to form a personality. The more conscious I am, the more aware I am of my own thoughts, the more monkey mind recedes. Eventually, words recede and thoughts recede. Ultimately, the retreat master tells me, meditation is an act of heightened consciousness, without words, a state of pure awareness, and can only occur on the path to enlightenment. Peace of mind is your birthright, kid, he says. It comes through awareness, and awareness comes through inner silence. You can only find it when you are awake, conscious, aware, ready to hand yourself over to it.

One of the Desert Fathers, Abbot Agatho, once lived with a stone in his mouth for three years to teach himself silence. Silence is the pearl of great price, the light cast on an unseen world. The deep places of the ocean are silent, yet there is life there. Zen master Genro said: "A cloud rests at the mouth of the cave doing nothing all day. The moonlight penetrates the waves throughout the night, but leaves no trace in the water."

By early afternoon, I had washed the dishes, vacuumed the cabin, scrubbed the car, picked a bucket of blackberries from a spot that the bear hadn't gotten to yet, jogged down the road toward Squilax until I was breathless, and, for the next ten minutes and fifteen seconds, watched the osprey diving for fish. Then I jogged back to the cabin, beat the pillows from the chesterfield until they were approximately clean; exhausted, I stood on the pier and watched the waves roll toward shore.

The problem with running away is that you take yourself with you. Wherever you go, you are already there. And it doesn't help with monkey mind, either, because monkey mind is the quintessential act of running away. Mastering the brain noise is the best way to find the freedom of enlightenment. Conquering it is conquering yourself, because monkey mind is the accumulation of every puff of insecurity, every screech of anger, every twist of pain, every whimper of despair. It is thought running away from itself, and you conquer it only when you stand fast, only when you say no more running, no more pretending. I will be here, now, as I am.

I wasn't a very good priest, I supposed, because I couldn't let go of other people's problems. Just let these things roll off you, my priest friends told me. Let them roll off like water off a new car. Most priests I know love new cars, because they're the only children they'll ever have. I once heard a bishop say about his Cadillac: Father can't fuck, so he has to buy his children. I thought of new cars, new Ford Mustangs, and driving down the road real fast, and then I thought of children playing in the road, and then I thought of babies being crushed to death in cars. You'll never survive in this business if you don't let these things roll off, my friends said. But I didn't know how. This was the first time I had been alone in a couple of days, and all the things I was scuttling away from rushed back at me. I prayed to be like Joe, who could watch a fire and be silent, free from pain, free from passion.

Breathe, I thought.

Breathe.

Zen master Joshu once asked a young monk whether he'd been here before. The monk said he had. Joshu said, "Have a cup of tea."

I watched a bird hopping along the shoreline, bathing itself in the cool water, fluttering its wings like thoughts. It stopped, cocked its head, chirped once, and cocked its head again, as if listening. I breathed deeply through my mouth, the wind of my breath roaring in my ears. My thoughts, fluttering inside, quieted; hopped back and forth, chirped once, and stopped. *Breathe.* I held the silence as long as I could—a minute, two, three, breathing into it and out of it. I breathed, and my arm itched. My back itched, right at that place I knew I couldn't scratch. Pray, I thought. I tried to think of something pious—the Virgin Mary, standing on the sun. I held that image for another three minutes, and then it transmogrified into my sister Teresa doing pious poses, like she used to do as a girl, her hands crossed over her chest, her eyes rolled heavenward, like Saint Agnes just before they cut off her head. Teresa could never hold that pose for more than two seconds before she broke down and giggled. And then she was at our swimming pool in Los

Angeles, in her swimming suit, doing pious poses, and then giggling, and then she was Marilyn Monroe, in a bathing suit, doing pious poses. I thought, Marilyn Monroe? And then Marilyn Monroe was naked, doing pious poses, and I shook my head to clear it. I had been through this before. I needed a cup of tea.

Groaning, I climbed out of the aluminum chair, creaking my stiff muscles up to the cabin, pulled out the electric teapot, and heated water. The tea filled me, gracious and sympathetic, slowing my brain to a friendly walk. Drinking hot tea is like having your shoulder squeezed by an old friend. Coffee gets you going; tea settles you down. It sets the world spinning in the right direction. My thoughts strolled by, dignified. I sipped more tea and rested my chin on an upturned palm. For the first time in two days, I felt the struggles melt away, my mind and heart settling into a comfortable peace. I suspected that I was failing the entire venture, failing at the internal life. I had failed at words, and was now failing at silence. Where could I go after that? My brain started revving again, so I took another slurp of tea, and everything calmed. Odd how peace, longed for, suddenly comes unbidden, out of some hidden place. How long it will stay is a mystery. My mind watches without desire, without need. I see the two worlds, inside and out, the fluttering of birds and the fluttering of thoughts, the nervous jerking of my insides, and I am suddenly able to watch without fear. My thoughts flow by like scenes in a movie. Voices come and go—angry, funny, stupid, accusing, lustful voices—and they seem part of a passing parade. These thoughts are a part of me, but they are also apart from me. I stand apart from them, detached, as if they belong to a world that comes and goes. The retreat master appears, this time in saffron robes and with a shaved head, but with the same cigar. That's it, kid, he said. That's what it feels like. This is the secret, kid. It's a parade, kid. The thoughts float by on the air; you see them, you feel them, you know they are there, but you don't let them take control. As long as you don't run away from them, they can't chase you. They're only fancies, ghosts, kid—let them pass, watch them pass, and they will.

I carried the cup of tea and my copy of D. T. Suzuki's *An Introduction to Zen Buddhism*, stuck it behind Helen Waddell's *The Desert Fathers*, and returned to the chair, edgy and guilt-ridden over bringing books with me. By that time, the morning had thinned toward noon, the shadows disengaging, and the first winds of the day ruffled my hair, hissing in the aspen trees behind me. White cumulus mounted the hills. I opened *The Desert Fathers*. Abbot Arsenius came to a place where the reeds were hissing in the wind, and he said, "What is that rustling?" and the monks said, "Just the reeds." And the old man said, "If a man sits quiet and hears so much as the voice of a bird, he has no real silence in his heart. How much worse will it be for you, who hear the sounds of these reeds?"

Crashing into despair, I shut the book and dropped it onto the deck of the pier. Who could be that detached? I was doomed, I told myself, cursed with a brain. This was too far beyond me, a perfection I could never achieve. My own brain was driving me crazy, but I knew that just being silent on the outside wasn't enough. I had to push on, because the silence had to be inside, too.

Thoreau wrote that for him to be alone, he had to avoid himself. "How could I be alone in the Roman emperor's chamber of mirrors?" he said. Me looking at me looking at me looking at me, an infinite regression of narcissism. An echo chamber, where a whisper is amplified to a shout, and I am deafened by my own voice. Kid, the retreat master said, You don't look so good.

When I was seven, I awakened from a dream I couldn't remember and knew that I was going to die. I tried to grasp the dream, pull it back into memory, but it slipped away, leaving only a touch of nausea. I didn't know when I would die, or how, and I hoped it would be a very long time away, but even so—I was going to die. The next two hours, I sat in bed clutching my pillow, watching the moonlight pool on the quilt and dribble onto the floor. Clouds cut pieces from the moon, dissolving them into silver-white fire. The light in my room dimmed, came back, and dimmed again, and it seemed as if the whole world was fading out and fading in. For many years after, clocks held both a certain fascination and a certain terror for me. Such precise ticking away of instants! Such minuscule subtractions from a life! Each tick was a second taken away, a second that would never come back. Not ever. Second by second, tick by tick, my life dripped away. This dying is ruining my life! I told my father, but he only laughed and patted me on the head.

Since that moment of epiphany, the fear has always been there, for the fear is fundamental. It emerges from the intuition that I am a creature, not responsible for my own existence; that I, too, come and go. It is the deepest fear of all, the fear that I am not quite real. As I have grown into adulthood, I have managed to keep it corralled by activity, but from time to time, I feel it pushing like a bear caged too long. Sometimes it emerges as a fear of death, sometimes as a fear of nascent evil. When I stop talking, when I stop doing, I am brought to that place where nightmares come wilding back. I did not make myself and therefore do not have the power to keep myself in existence. There are those in the sciences who think that I am a biological machine, a pattern of tissue, a swirl of matter, brought together for a moment only in time to swirl away. Perhaps this is so. Others claim that I am an illusion, a puff of ego eventually carried off on the wind. Whatever I am is hidden from me. I live behind a mask. Am I the face behind the mask or the mask itself? As Jorge Luis Borges wrote about his own dreams, "These are my most terrible nightmares: I see myself reflected in a mirror, but the reflection is wearing a mask. I am afraid to pull the mask off, afraid to see my real face, which I imagine to be hideous. There may be leprosy or evil or something more terrible than anything I am capable of imagining."

The mask haunts me, the mirror haunts me, the clock haunts me—my existence feels ghostly, like a subatomic particle that pops into being one instant and pinches out the next. I am terrifyingly mutable. What will I be tomorrow? I call to mind the stories of evil men who were good and decent in childhood, and somehow became twisted into killers. What dark potentials lie in the deep seas of my unconscious? Do I have the courage to remove the mask?

I breathed. I breathed to find peace, which came in bits, short moments of quiet punctuating long quarter hours of noise. But my breath was fearful, and it did no good. The voices, the pictures never fled, but were merely pushed to one side, sullen, crowded into a corner, waiting for a break in vigilance to rush brawling back. I paced the beach, then, finally exhausted by my own company, packed myself into the car and drove to Squilax, over the bridge, and down to Chase, to the market to buy fish, or cereal, or milk, or anything, just to talk to another human being for one bloody second.

I parked across the street from the store, crossed over, and hurried inside.

Hello, hello, hello, Father, the owner's wife said to me as I passed by. She was a wide woman, short, and moved from side to side as she walked. Whenever she met me, she wiped her hands on her apron, as if she had a guilty conscience. As you see, she said, we are awfully quiet these days, pointing widely at the empty store.

No more tourists, I said, smiling at her, glad of another human voice.

Now I can relax, she said. The man and I are going down to the States after the first snow. He has a sister down there. I can't stand her, but she's family. Sometimes I think she hates me. She's never nice, but I think that comes from living in California. And her children! Such monsters! Aren't you from California, Father? Everyone's crazy down there, they say.

Sounds like fun, I said, saving up my answers for a single burst. I'm sorry about your sister-in-law, and yes, I'm from California. And yes, everyone is crazy down there.

She followed me to the fish counter, where I picked over the salmon steaks, and all the while told me about her sister-in-law, whose husband runs a little grocery in Rancho Cucamonga, and that her sister-in-law was a grasping, difficult woman who takes after her mother, another grasping, difficult woman. It's in the blood, they say, and wasn't she lucky that the man took after his father, who was a kind, decent man, and why these kind, decent men fall for grasping, difficult women she didn't know, but it always seemed to work out that way.

I glanced at her sidelong, wondering if she understood the implications of everything she was saying. Then I picked out a healthy salmon steak and scuttled back to the front register, with her still carrying on. She told me about how unruly the tourists had been that summer, and now that they were gone it was so *quiet* around the place, except for all the Indians who hung around in the store, never buying anything, acting as if they were waiting for something. I glared at her, remembering her treatment of Joe a few days before, but she didn't seem to notice. Then she returned to the subject of her in-laws—not the ones in California this time, but the ones in Toronto, the ones who made their own wine and their own beer, and even tried their hand at vodka, which they liked a little too much to her way of thinking. When she started on her mother-in-law, a grasping and difficult woman, I wondered what it was I had missed so much when I was back at the cabin, and what it was I had needed so very much to hear. I paid for the fish, backing toward the door with the bag in hand, nodding as she went on and on and on, waved to her as the pneumatic door, something that she and the man were very proud of, shushed open behind me, and I backed out and hurried to my car.

Once inside, I breathed. Pushed to the edge, I began to let things go, like a fist opening, and I let thoughts drop from me one at a time. Clearing a space in my mind, I left it empty, breathing into it all the while, filling it with light. Silence formed while thoughts passed by, keeping their distance. The silence gathered as if on its own power, a silence without desperation, a silence that did not subvert me, but was me. As the noise, inside and out, retreated, and my brain calmed like a child falling asleep on the backseat of a car, awareness sharpened, whittling the blurred edges of the world into fine lines. I could not explain what had happened, nor could I make it happen again by force of will. Something like the rusty lid of a mason jar twisted free, and a new place inside of me opened. For five minutes, I had no mind at all—no thought, no desire for thought, no words, no analysis of problems, no desperate plans, no secret wishes, no self-flagellation, no neurotic itchiness. I was aware only of my breathing, my heartbeat, the touch of my fingers on my legs, the weight of my back and legs on the seat of the car. Then, abruptly, the car rocked, and something tapped on the closed window, breaking the silent space. The owner's wife stood at the car window, holding a piece of paper in her hand.

You forgot your receipt, she said.

I opened the window and took it from her. Thanks, I said.

Are you all right?

I'm fine. I was just—thinking.

She looked at me sideways, as if thinking itself were suspect. All right, she said, and walked back to the store.

Turning down the twisting dirt road to the cabin, I felt the silence waiting for me there, but this time it felt palpable, fearful. Yet it also held a possibility I had not felt before. But would it last? I took the salmon steak out of the bag and perused it. My first plan had been to roll out the barbecue grill stored underneath the screened-in porch, scrub it clean, and cook the salmon for myself. A little indulgence. But the afternoon had slowly deepened into evening, and though I could list almost nothing that I had actually done that day, I felt exhausted, as if I had done a long day's work under the hot sun. But this wasn't the comfortable exhaustion of flesh and bone, but of heart and soul. It was an exhaustion of the mind.

I tucked the salmon, bag and all, into the refrigerator, drained the last gulp of aging milk before it finally turned, and stood at the sink, eating tuna out of the can. As the sun fell and the evening settled, my brain settled with it. I felt like sighing, as if I was sighing with the whole world. My thoughts quieted and fluttered about and then composed themselves for sleep. I stretched out on the porch lounger. My mind was finally at peace, but a peace that came partly from stupefaction. Loons warbled on the other side of the lake. A wheat train thrummed up the mountain to the pass. As I drifted toward sleep, my old habit of worrying about people got the better of me, and I started fretting about Albert with his car still stuck at the garage. Had he gotten home all right? My brain was starting to take off again.

The stars dusted the sky with light, sparkling and winking and scintillating. The moon, nearly full, pushed over the tops of the mountains down the long length of the big lake, mounting higher until it was all the way up, its reflection twisting in the water. Unbidden, the image of an infant crushed to death by a boulder falling in slow motion off a cliff beat into the silence, and I found myself weeping, not just for the baby, but for the mother, and for the father, and for myself, and for Joe, and for Albert, and for Mrs. Mouncy, and for Nora Cooper, and for the whole wide stupid world. Just let it roll off your back, they said; but it wasn't on my back, it was inside me, so far inside that it felt like a bullet buried in a lung, one I would have to use forceps to dig out. The mother's eyes appeared, and that single question was still in them: Why? And my answer was the same: I don't know.

And then suddenly I knew the truth, the truth that not even the retreat master could tell me, the truth that only God could tell me—that I was enraged with God Himself, that bastard, that monster, for killing a child, and for never even leaving a note. Nothing but silence. Inside my head, the father and mother trapped in the car screamed *Why?* at me. I was in the father's place, beating my hands against the wheel, tears streaming down my cheeks, tearing at the door, then trying to comfort my wife, who was also screaming, and failing that, screaming again. *Why? Why?* rocked back and forth. Jesus, I thought, if I don't stop this, I'll go nuts for sure. It would be a long night.

Six

I'VE BEEN READING THOREAU again. The vast majority of humankind, he says, lives on the surface, like froth on the sea. They float, bobbing in the swells, rushing in and out with the tide, focusing on the world, on work, on politics, on the gathering of power, and on the acquisition of wealth. They are creatures of circumstance, blind to truth. I am one of these. I have lived, as Thoreau said, between my eyeballs and the tip of my nose. I am used to it. I run on automatic, uncritical, unthinking, unconscious, accepting the values of my society, good or bad, believing what I am told to believe about life, about myself, worrying about what I am told to worry about. I have a calendar and I jot things in it. I think of myself as a project, a work. Make something of yourself, son, my father said. I've been trying. I really have.

The word "obsession" comes from the Latin *obsidere,* "to possess," which in turn comes from *ob-sedere,* "to sit on." Now and then, a thought can possess the mind, sit on it, driving out everything else. An image of a stack of paper waiting for me on my desk at the parish collided with a snapshot of the mother's head resting on the chrome railing at the hospital. I willed it gone, like someone yelling at a barking dog—Stop it! Stop it! Stop it!

I was tired of struggling, tired of making war on myself. A couple of days of trying to contemplate seemed like years and years. All for five minutes of awareness in my car and the realization that I was pissed off at God. It didn't feel worth it. Why not ignore the whole thing and wait for it to go away? Why not give up? Wouldn't it be easier to go back to the parish? I was screwing it up, anyway. There's nothing so bad that I can't run away from it if I try. That's life, I told myself. Ordinary, average life. It's what everybody does. So what's wrong with that? What's wrong with keeping busy all the time? Hard work. Nose to the grindstone. Suddenly, the retreat master was there, cigar and all. He said to me: So if everybody jumps off a bridge, kid, are you going to jump off, too? I said: You sound like my mom. He said: What you're talking about isn't living, kid—it's existing; it's killing time. You want to go back to sleep? You want to float through life? Why? Because it's too hard to wake up? Waking up means struggle, pain, suffering, and you don't like those things. He puffed meaningfully on his cigar. So who does? he said after a moment. Nobody. But it's the only way. You have to dig into yourself like a gold miner looking for the big strike. And you will find it, in time. It's the Mystery, kid, the Mystery that, once found, exists in every moment. But if you don't find it, your life passes unconsciously and the moments slip by unaware. People who are asleep wait for miracles and are disappointed every day. People who are awake know that life itself is a miracle. People who are awake see wonder at every moment, in every fold of the world. They are alive, aware of their life, aware of their actions, aware of the movements of their hearts. Most people just don't understand this. They don't understand how astounding "ordinary" is. If you want to wake up, kid, you have to wrestle with yourself, free yourself. You have to grow up, and that part hurts. You don't have to make something of yourself to be someone, kid.

So I stay. I stay, still worried, still uncertain, still fearful. I stay for now, for today, though I might leave tomorrow. The dappled sun is bright, while the air feels cooler, heavier. New weather coming. A marshy smell has wafted off the lake as the humidity swells. The sparrows hush, the fish hide on the bottom, the mosquitoes hardly circle, as if the entire valley waits.

Shutting my eyes from the sun, I wait. I'm not sure what I am waiting for—for God, for satori, for peace of soul, for the balance between sleep and waking to shift enough for me to climb out of the lounger. Luckily, I have a volume of Thomas Merton on the floor, so I fumble for it, open one eye, thumb through the book until I find a page. Merton says: "The only way to find solitude is by hunger and thirst and sorrow and poverty and desire, and the man who has found solitude is empty, as if he had been emptied by death." Great. More suffering. To heck with Merton, I say, and pick up *The Desert Fathers:* "An elder saw a certain one laughing and said to him: In the presence of the Lord of heaven and earth we must answer for our whole life, and you can laugh?" That sucks, too. It's a conspiracy. The books are against me. Why can't I find a spiritual writer who will say, "Party hearty, and you will be saved"? They all want me to sit, suffer through the tornado, and *wait.* I hate waiting.

The week after my ordination, I flew to LA to see family and stumbled across an old high school buddy on the street. He was in sales then and they were starting a new line of luxury cars, and it was going to be *big,* and gosh they were excited about it. Three years later, I met him once more at a party. He introduced his wife, who was friendly, but whose tight eyes hinted at anger simmering under the surface. While we spoke, he boused two rum-and-Cokes and was reaching for a third when his wife put her hand on his arm and looked at him. He laughed; then, his voice quavering, he said, "Maybe I'll just have the Coke," and left. His wife and I glanced at each other uncomfortably. When he returned, he continued the conversation at exactly the place he had left it. He was with a new firm now, a computer company, and they were introducing a new line of monitors, and they were sure these would be *big*, and gosh they were really excited about it.

The Talmud says: "Study with all your heart and soul that you may know God's ways and be attentive to His Torah. Guard His Torah in your heart and keep the fear of Him before your eyes. Guard your lips from every sin, and purify and sanctify yourself from fault and wrong-doing. And God will be with you everywhere." You can do this even in a busy world if you keep your wits about you. And wits are exactly what are needed—keenness of perception, calmness under fire, perspective, and the grace to keep all things in right order. One after another, I have seen men and women of good soul fail at happiness because they were too busy trying to make something of themselves. They ran from mania to despair. Eventually, they looked for a reason to get up in the morning and couldn't find one. A month after the party, I received a letter from the high school buddy, who asked me, What's the point? I didn't have an answer for him then, because I didn't know what the point was, either.

"Hold every moment sacred," Thomas Mann says. "Hold fast the time! Watch over it, every hour, every minute! Unregarded it slips away, like a lizard, smooth, slippery, faithless, a pixie wife." Time well loved reaches past bare reason, and binds you to the universe second by second, over-stuffed with pith and purpose. When my mind is asleep, I stretch myself over the landscape, arms, legs, fingers and toes, ears and hair pulled tightly from my body. A great rubber man, I flatten and spindle, drawn by useless entertainments and questionable obligations. When my mind is awake, I gather myself into one contained body in one specific place and time, and there practice the art of silence, and attend to the holiness of the world. For every human being, at every age, in every tuck and pleat of the world, there is either enlightenment or madness. I place before you life and death, Moses said. Choose life. Even as a priest, I lived madly, and did so because it was easier. I played at sainthood, clat-tered through life when I should have been standing, still as a yearling fawn, learning to see. I diddled away the spiritual life, wasted the time, let it flow in and out of my hands like money, never once clenching tightly, and it was gone. Be thin, be confident, be successful, I told myself. Be in control, get in shape, work on your biceps, learn snappy byplay, understand the world of human beings. No wonder I was quivering with confusion my first few days of retreat. A wonder I hadn't melted down like a nuclear reactor and burned my way to China.

When I was ten, my parents relented and bought me a dog. She was a collie mix puppy who followed me everywhere and seemed to listen when I talked to her. I wanted to learn as much about her as I could. So I biked to the local library and checked out a big book on dogs. It was a very big book with glossy pictures of collies and German shepherds and chows and Chihuahuas. Heads cocked, big tongues hanging out—good old dogs. I comprehended the breed categories, the grooming tips, even the murky part about whelping puppies. But the chapter on dog intelligence baffled me. The difference between a dog and a human, the book said, is that a human is conscious and a dog is not. This had to be wrong. My dog seemed conscious enough to me—she was moving around, watching birds, barking at cars. Besides, I wanted my dog to be conscious, too, so we could be conscious together. So I went to my mother, big book in hand and dog in tow.

Are dogs conscious? I said to her. My mother looked up from her magazine, the gears shifting in her head. She looked at my dog, who seemed to be listening, and then looked at me.

Well, no, she said, they aren't. Not like people are conscious, anyway. Why?

I heaved the book onto the kitchen table and fingered the offending line.

If dogs aren't conscious, what are they?

Dogs are sort of conscious, she said. They're not conscious like people but they aren't unconscious, either. If that makes sense.

I looked at my dog, who cocked her head, as if pondering. Uh-huh, I said.

So it's all clear now?

Uh-uh.

My mother put her magazine on the table and folded her hands. Well, she said, dogs are not self-conscious, and people are. Dogs know things, and want things, but they don't know that they know it, or know that they want it. So they're conscious, but not self-conscious. Does that make sense?

Uh-huh.

So you understand it now?

Uh-uh.

Well, dogs aren't self-conscious, and that means they don't know as much as you do. They don't know how to talk. They don't know how to add or subtract, or how to read a book, or even how to pretend. Only people know how to pretend. Do you get it now?

Oh, I said.

My mother looked at me. You didn't understand a word I said, did you?

No, I said. I didn't understand, nor did I want to. My dog was conscious. She just was.

Well, don't worry about it, my mother said. You'll figure it all out sooner or later.

I never did, but for the next three days I tried my best to be as self-conscious as I could. Whenever I stood, I said to myself: Now I Am Standing, and whenever I sat, I said to myself: Now I Am Sitting Down. Somehow, my posture improved. When you are fully conscious, you have to have perfect posture, with elbows splayed, hands halfway in the air and pinky fingers erect, like a mannequin. I walked gingerly around the house as if I were carrying a book on my head. Now I Am Washing the Dishes, I told myself. Now I Am Washing a Spoon. Now I Am Washing a Fork. Now I Am Drying the Spoon. Now I Am Drying the Fork. I exhausted myself with this pretty quickly, but figured that this was only fair. I was self-conscious and my dog wasn't, and therefore I had to be as self-conscious as I could, self-conscious enough for both of us, and that meant being self-conscious all the time. My searchlight beams, inner and outer, had to be turned on twenty-four hours a day. No halfway measures—I owed that to the dog.

The Buddha says: A monk, when walking, knows that he is walking; when standing, knows that he is standing; when sitting, knows that he is sitting; when lying down, knows that he is lying down. Consciousness is always consciousness of something, and it is the *of* that makes all the difference. If I am conscious of a memory, then my mind circumambulates the past, somewhere where the memory is. If I am conscious of a hope, a plan, a dream, then I am abroad in the future, meandering in some possible world that might or might not come true. In both cases, my mind is elsewhere, far from my body, in a place where my body can't go. I am absentminded. And I am split, body and soul, sleepwalking. The only way to awaken is to reel that consciousness back into my own body, to wash the dishes for the sake of washing the dishes, to be aware of where I am and what I am doing at each moment of the day.

I am lying on the porch lounger, I tell myself as I stare at the spiderwebs on the ceiling. I am deciding to get up. *Right now* I am deciding to get up. Admittedly, my hands are still folded on my chest, I tell myself, and I haven't moved, not one inch, but even so, I have decided. I am getting up now. Yes, I am getting up. Where's my coffee? And even though there is still no movement, I will get up, now. I am aware of getting up. Now! Get up, now! I say. I grunt, then abandon myself to the day. I roll off the lounger and stand, my legs still shaky from the torpidity of the night. I feel like a lizard in need of a hot rock. When the Mr. Coffee stops dripping, I dig through the dishes on the sink, looking for a clean cup. No luck. Two fingers, a dribble of Ivory Liquid, a swish of water. Rubbing the porcelain in a circular motion with my thumb. The porcelain is slippery smooth, soapy wet, warm underneath the hot water from the tap. A smile-shaped chip on the rim breaks the smoothness of the glaze, rough under my thumb.

Consciousness is consciousness of something. I pick up the cup, name it, wash it, scrub it, put it away. I have a name for each piece, ready to go: cup, bowl, dish, spoon. I fix a word to the thing, and then think I know the thing, and then I put it on the shelf and move on to something else. If I were fully awake, I would wash the cup and leave the name on the shelf. I would place no names between the cup and my thumb, because without the names, the cup as it is would be in my hands. The mystery of its existence would be there, in the warm soapy smoothness, in the roughness of the chip. All the connections would be there, for the cup is made of stars and all the laws of the universe are holding its molecules together. I think this but know that these thoughts are only more names, and so let them flow by. I feel the cup. It is smooth. It is warm and soapy. All my thoughts are fixed on the cup, and on my thumb rubbing circles on the porcelain. With each swirl, more of the unspeakable universe is implicated in my thumb, folded into the simple act of washing the cup. I am completely myself, completely here in this place, washing this cup. My mind is fully here, and I am mindful of the cup and of the moment of washing. I am not in the future nor in the past. I am living this moment fully, this one moment. The wonder of existence is here, now. All the rest is fantasy.

Mindfulness is as simple as this: When walking, be aware that you are walking. When sitting, be aware that you are sitting. When washing the cup, be aware that you are washing the cup. Leave the head noise for another day; let it pass like traffic in the city. Starve it out; leave it nothing to feed on, nothing to clutch, nothing to hold. Make your mind as smooth, wet, and soapy as the porcelain beneath your thumb. Monkey mind will unwind, calm itself; it will sit in one place, silent, serene as the Buddha.

After three cups of coffee, I took a walk up to the road. A goldfinch fluttered past, landed on a branch, and darted away on some other business. A knot of vesper sparrows dove and climbed, wheeled and whirled, picking mosquitoes out of the air. Two ducks banked over the lake, wings open, and, in perfect formation, stuck their legs out, splashed down, coasted. A buck mule deer broke through the undergrowth beside the road about twenty feet from me and sashayed to the middle of the road, followed by a brace of does. They stopped, looked at me, heads turning in perfect sync. Not wanting to break the spell, I turned away from them, pretended not to care. All four of us were frozen in place, like a tableau. The moment hushed me. I was simply there with the deer, watching them sideways as they watched me. I stuck my hands into my pockets and meditated on the lake. After a few seconds, I bent down and pretended to be looking for something in the grass, moving the grassy stalks one way then another as if I had lost a contact lens. Eventually, the deer forgot me. They must have decided that I was no threat and changed me into a piece of scenery. They browsed by the side of the road, pulling up stalks of grass, munching the tender shoots. Eventually, one of the does nibbled in my direction. I pulled a handful of grass and tossed it in her path. She noshed that, so I pulled out some more, and she noshed that, too. I felt like Saint Francis of Assisi. The seconds flowed one into another as the doe wandered closer, until I could nearly reach out and stroke her flank. Suddenly, the male poked up his head, ears twitching, and turned toward the road. A few seconds after, I heard the faint sound of a Jeep. The three deer bolted for the thick underbrush. Five seconds later, the Jeep passed, the driver chugging a can of Molson's and playing Canadian country and western extra loud.

Walking toward the cabin, I swam through a cloud of dust kicked up by the Jeep. On the way down, I heard the sound of children and then a woman shouting. Annie was sitting on the cabin steps, smoking a cigarette; two of her children ran around the open space where my car stood, while Tommy, nearly ten, stood in the boat and rocked it back and forth as violently as he could, trying to swamp it.

Trouble? I said.

Annie shrugged and dragged on her cigarette. Same as always, she said.

Rehab didn't take, I said.

Annie puffed, shook her head infinitesimally.

Why don't you leave the son of a bitch? I said.

Annie shrugged one shoulder. She was somewhere between one-quarter and one-eighth Shuswap, and I was never sure whether she had enough blood in her to make the rolls. She and her children were shadows that walked between the worlds, neither one nor the other, tainted on both sides. Each child was fathered by a different boyfriend soon gone, but never without taking a bite out of Annie's spirit. Whenever she had trouble, Annie showed up on my door. Like the deer, she must have thought I was safe. She was pretty, with high Indian cheekbones, dark hair, blue eyes, in her twenties. She'd had her first child, a boy, when she was fourteen, but he'd died mysteriously. When disgusted, she went to her sister's house so the two of them could complain together. When afraid, she came to me—simply, without warning, children in tow. I never understood how she knew where I was. I didn't mind Annie too much; when she wanted to talk, she talked, when she didn't want to talk, she didn't. Usually, she sat by herself, staring at the water, while her kids ran wild, until one of them screamed, and then she mounted like a thunderstorm, screaming back, slapping.

Is Peter with you? I said. If Annie was an irritant, her brother Peter was a problem. He had recently spent a year in prison for nearly beating his wife and son to death.

Annie shrugged again. He may show up, she said. You know Peter. I never can tell how he finds me.

Probably the same way you find me, I said. A smile flickered across her face. She reached into a plastic grocery bag beside her and pulled out a whole sockeye.

Who caught that? I said.

My Uncle Peter, she said. He gave it to me and said I should give it to you.

That's a lot of fish.

Annie smiled wholeheartedly this time. It's a good thing you got company, she said.

Yeah, good thing. I took the salmon from her and led her into the kitchen. She shouted at the kids before she came in, and then stood by me, tamping out her cigarette on a clean saucer, and in one motion pulled out her box of Craven As and lit a fresh one. It was then that I noticed a bruise on her right cheek and puffiness around her right eye. I put my fingers up to the bruise, but she turned away. There's ice in the fridge, I said. She shook her head no and puffed on her cigarette.

Just after noon I discovered Annie sitting in the aluminum chair by the floating dock, intently burning the skin of her forearm with the hot button of the cigarette. I plucked it from her and finger-flicked it into the lake. Annie looked up at me blankly. In twisty, chaotic ways, Annie was a devotee of death. The war inside, the divided self. The choice is before each of us at every single turn of life. How long Annie had been at war with her flesh, I didn't know. Poor flesh. It wants such simple things—it sleeps too much, it eats too much, it watches too much TV, it thinks constantly about sex. It gets colds. It farts. It likes beer, and after a good beer, it likes to burp. At war with our own flesh, we each of us invent reasons to feel guilty. We fall madly in love, we fall madly out of love, we fall madly into depression, we feel mysteriously elated, and we feel sudden shame for stupid reasons. True darkness begins inside. Freud called it the death instinct. Augustine called it original sin. It is that unspeakable urge toward death, that impulse toward self-immolation. Who can say where it began or what function it serves in human life? Who can say why we have it at all? It is simply there, a fact of life, like cancer.

The wars that humans perpetrate begin inside, an outward expression of the catapult barrages of the heart. William James divided the range of human souls into two types: healthy-minded and sick-minded. Healthy-minded people see the world as good, and themselves as good in it. They find ways to see good in life and to increase the good of others. Sick-minded people see the world as evil, a place of anguish where guilt is the norm and sin is on every side. They actively find ways to discover more sin, and more anguish, and if told otherwise, will accuse the speaker of being a soft-minded fool. Most people are somewhere in between, healthy-minded on some days and sick-minded on others. I am most sick-minded when I am angry. I'm a big guy and all my life I've been told that angry big guys are ipso facto bullies, so I have avoided anger, stuffed it down my own throat until suddenly it vomits forth. Anger begets fear, fear begets self-loathing, self-loathing begets perpetual shame. Each iteration folds inside the one before until the warfare disappears, quivering among the atoms. My mood plummets. I become another person, whiny, irritable, miserable, and I don't know why.

At some level, I knew that Annie was abusing my good nature, and I was angry about it, but I also knew that she was a wandering soul who needed some fixed point in her life, a quiet anchorage to find sanity. Her life was out of control, caught up by the whirlwind. What made me most angry, however, was that I could do nothing substantive to help her. I couldn't fix her life, because it wasn't mine to fix. Grunting surrender, I walked up to the cabin and pulled a fish knife out of the drawer near the sink, and cut the salmon down the belly, lengthwise, cleaned out the guts, cut off the head, boned it, and cut the meat into fillets. Cutting hard, chopping hard, cooking with rage.

You're good, Annie said, appearing suddenly at my side, but not as good as my Uncle Peter.

Well, I've been fishing as long as you've been alive, I said. And your Uncle Peter's been fishing as long as I've been alive.

Leaving the fillets on the counter, I stepped out of the cabin, followed by Annie, and pulled the old barbecue grill out from under the porch and filled it with fresh briquettes, piling them into a pyramid, and dousing them with lighter fluid. At first, the flame burned high, leaving a metallic, oily taste in the air, but then it died back and burned inward, sullen. The kids gathered around and made noises, the littlest girl edging too close. I put my hand on her shoulder and pulled her back; startled, she looked at me with big eyes, and then hid behind her mother.

Let's let these cook for a while, I said, something my father always said whenever he first lit the briquettes. For the next ten minutes, Annie and I and the children stared transfixed at the briquettes as they whitened around the edges. Tommy was the first to break, running down to the pier, toward the boat and more trouble.

Don't swamp that boat! I shouted after him.

He turned and looked at me, defiant, but then sat on the pier and threw rocks at the water. When the briquettes were ready, I placed the fillets neatly around the grill. Annie stayed indoors, poked around inside of the refrigerator and the cabinets, and came out a few minutes later, announcing that we had salad and baked beans.

The salmon was nearly done when I turned to say something to Annie and found Peter standing behind me, a cigarette in one corner of his mouth and a bottle of beer in his hand. He was wearing a baseball cap that said "Bullshit!" on the front.

Finish that beer and throw the bottle away, I said. In the trash can, please. That's the last beer you'll have for a while, because I got no more around here.

He nodded, puffed on his cigarette, scratched his neck with his fingers.

There's Coke in the fridge, though.

He nodded again, chugged the last of the beer, dropped it in the trash, and started for the cabin for a can of Coke. I was glad I hadn't bought any beer at the liquor store. Peter was a mean drunk. Once the year before when they were all visiting me at the cabin, he had brought his own bottle of bad Scotch and drank it all, and then suggested that I take Annie to bed, because, well, she'd sleep with anybody. Annie ducked her head, going turtle while he talked, until he grabbed her. She screamed and pushed him away. He went back for her again, so I picked him up, threw him over my shoulder, and carried him outside, up the road, with him screaming and punching at me all the way. When we got to the top of the hill, I dumped him unceremoniously onto the dirt road, and told him to lose himself, anywhere but here. He stood and tried to lunge at me, but he was too drunk. I tripped him and he landed on his stomach. I knelt on his back and pushed his head into the dirt.

Now Peter, I told him. I've got a hundred pounds on you, and most of it is muscle. I'm a lot stronger than you, and I don't want any violence in this cabin. So go away and sober up.

After I let him up, he stood, brushed off his jeans with his baseball cap, and after glaring at me a while, started down the road.

And have some respect for your sister! I called after him. He said nothing but kept walking. The next time I saw him, he couldn't remember a thing. But that was a year before, and Peter's memory had been growing potholes along the way. He was usually violent only when he was drunk, and then only when he was drunk enough. Each time I happened upon him, he seemed puzzled, as if we had some history but he couldn't remember what it was.

Peter remained sober all that afternoon and evening. Because I had no beer around the house, he had no choice. Annie sat on the steps, cigarette in hand; the kids ran around the car, screaming and laughing, while Peter stood beside me and stared into the fire, cigarette in one hand, Coke in the other.

Do you think I'm possessed? he said.

How's that?

He looked me in the eye, in earnest. Possessed. Possessed by the devil, he said.

Why do you say that?

He looked down at the fire. I just got out of jail, you know.

I know.

I don't even remember doing it. They just tell me I did it.

Uh-huh. I flipped the salmon over and watched the fire with him.

She's taken up with some other guy now. And my boy won't even talk to me.

I'm sorry to hear that, I said, counting another pothole in Peter's memory.

I don't know what happened. Why I beat them. She said she was in hospital for weeks afterward. He looked at his shoes. I don't know, he said.

I said nothing, just nodded.

So am I possessed?

I looked at him, remembered a time two years before, a time Peter never remembered. I was doing a funeral at the reservation church, waiting for the people to show up with the body. I usually arrived at the church early to set up the altar and get things ready, while the body was at the Community Center for the wake. The people walked from there to the church, a mile on a dirt road, following the hearse.

I was standing that day on the front steps of the church, waiting for them to come, fretting because I hate waiting, when Peter rode up on a tall bay horse. He was drunk. He slid off the saddle, steadied himself against the horse's flank, tied the horse to the bumper of an abandoned car, and staggered over to me. Apparently, he had determined that day to kill himself a white man, and since there was nobody else around, he figured that I would do. Trying to tell him that he was mostly white himself would have been useless. I waited on the steps until he approached me, and then he pulled out a .38 he had tucked into his belt, pointed it right at my nose, and held it as steady as he could.

I'm going to kill you, white man, he said.

I looked down the barrel of the gun.

Peter, I said, if you kill a priest, you know that the ground will open up at that moment and swallow you, and you will go straight to hell. Immediately. To hell with theology, I thought.

The gun wavered in Peter's hand. Without a word, he dropped the gun to his side, tucked it into his belt, and staggered to his horse. He was too drunk to climb up, so he untied the horse and slowly led it away.

That was two years before, and Peter never remembered any of it. I looked at him, trying to find an answer to his question. I left the smoking grill and walked to the trash can, pulled open the steel top, reached for the empty beer bottle, and held it up to him, then dropped it back in. Yeah, Peter, I said. You're possessed. But not by what you think.

Not by the devil?

Well, maybe, sort of. They don't call it spirits for nothing.

He nodded, and his face bunched up. He wept soundlessly, tears running down his cheeks. Annie looked at him, sadness in her eyes. She moved over to him and stood next to him without touching him. I put my hand on his shoulder and squeezed.

I get so confused, he said. Things just keep going on, and most of the time, I don't even remember it. Things just seem to go on, and I don't have any control over them. I just keep doing the same damn things over and over, he said.

I looked at him and squeezed his shoulder one more time. Sadness and fellow feeling invaded my years of anger with him, and I saw him revealed, terrified, a lost child. How different were we after all? All that noise. All that confusion. Peter and Annie and I stood around the fire, our common humanity leaking through our skin, one to the other, pouring one to the next while Peter wept.

Running on automatic, I told him. He looked up, wiped his tears, and nodded.

Seven

PETER SULKED THROUGH THE afternoon, sitting at the end of the pier, away from everyone else while we ate. For the next three hours, he smoked one cigarette after another, flicking the smoldering nubs into the lake and lighting another, until five o'clock, when he ran out and bummed off his sister. The two of them killed her pack fifteen minutes later and Peter was at me, begging to borrow my car to drive into town for a few packs of Craven As. I shot him the look.

Peter, I said, you don't want to borrow my car. You'd go with the best intentions, I'm sure, and believe that you were only going to buy smokes, and you would buy them, but then you'd say, One beer wouldn't hurt—and you'd buy one beer, which would mean that you'd have to buy two beers, and pretty soon, you'd forget whose car you were driving, and you'd run off with it, and get drunk someplace, and I'd have to hunt you down, and pull my car out of a ditch, and the rest would be uncomfortable for both of us. There would be yelling and accusations and begging for mercy. It wouldn't be pretty.

Peter held his hands up, innocent. I'm just going for some smokes.

Uh-huh, I said. Peter, there's a better chance of pigs whistling the "Ode to Joy" in four-part harmony than there is of you getting behind the wheel of my car. A much better chance.

Drive me, then, he said. I've got to have some cigarettes.

You can do without them for a while.

I need some, too, Annie said. He took all mine.

Couldn't you do without them, too?

Annie looked at me as if the thought had never occurred to her, or could ever occur to her. Then the kids ran up from the lakefront, screaming that they wanted ice cream. I looked at Peter, then at Annie, then at the kids.

I need money, I said.

Peter and Annie glanced at each other and dug into their pockets, coming up with $2.50 between them. In change. I could see it coming; the rest of the bill was mine.

Six of us climbed out of my car just as the market owner's wife was sweeping out the store for the night. Peter pounded on the glass door, and she came to see who it was, saw Peter, then Annie and the kids, and shook her head no. Then she saw me in the back and unlocked the door, smiling and welcoming us in an obsequious shopkeeper voice.

Father! It's good to see you. You were here just yesterday.

This is true, I said. And now I'm back. I pointed to the rest of the crowd, my finger tracing out a circle in the air, as if to lasso them all. They're here for cigarettes. I'm not. They're here for ice cream. That, I'll do, but I'm here mainly for Cokes.

All right, she said. But I'm just getting ready to close, and the man is expecting me home to cook dinner, so you'll have to hurry.

I looked at all my sudden guests and gave them the evil eye. We will, I said.

From there, I walked back to the cooler while the kids squealed all the way to the ice cream freezer and returned with a half gallon of chocolate mocha fudge something with nuts. Annie disappeared, followed by Peter, who whispered to her all the way to the back of the store. Three or four minutes later, we gathered at the registers. Annie pulled the change she and Peter had put together and jingled it onto the counter. The shopkeeper's wife sized up the purchases—a half gallon of ice cream, a six-pack of Cokes, four packs of Craven As, a loaf of bread, and a half-dozen eggs—then looked at Annie, who looked at me.

I'll take care of the rest, I said. She nodded, rang it up. The bill came to $14.45. I reached for my wallet, and suddenly Tommy quietly placed three bottles of Molson Ale onto the counter alongside the Cokes.

Take those off, Tommy, I said. He looked at his Uncle Peter, then at his mother, then at me, and didn't move. I stared at Peter. No bloody way, Peter, I said.

Father! the shopkeeper's wife said.

I kept my eyes on Peter. I repeat, I said. Peter, no damned bloody way! The shopkeeper's wife's eyes were wide, and her hand was at her mouth. Didn't she think priests could swear? I thought. Peter stuck his fingers in his jeans, turned away, stamped his foot like a child, and swore back. No one else moved to take the bottles away, so I pushed them to one side and paid for the rest. Tommy helped bag the groceries. The shopkeeper's wife smiled at him and pinched his cheek. Such a nice boy, she said, and looked balefully at me. It seemed that I had fallen from grace.

As we were leaving the store, I leaned toward Annie. You're not helping him at all, you know.

He said he needed it, she told me, then turned red and looked away.

I'm sure he thinks that, I said. But it's killing him.

Peter didn't speak to me on the way home, didn't speak to me all the rest of that day. His hands shook as he lit his cigarettes, one after the other, as the sun set behind the mountains. I watched him sadly until he moved down to the dockside and sat in the aluminum chair, staring at the lake while the loons called. Evening settled to blue, then intensified to black. I glanced at Peter's back as the shadows pooled together and darkness thickened, wondering if I had looked as forlorn sitting in that same spot the day before. Annie followed the kids outside and sat with them on the pebble shore while Tommy threw rocks at the water. Alone for the first time that day, I gathered the dishes from the afternoon's barbecue, and humming tunelessly, washed them in the sink, one at a time, trying intently with each dish to wash it for its own sake. Instead, I found myself scrubbing harder and harder, as if to wear off the glaze. My humming had become a low, animal growl. Settled in each person's psyche like subterranean rock is a layer where anger gets buried. With time, the weight of the overburden churns the nearby psyche into an angry magma. The only way to keep it buried there is to continue putting pressure on it, but that heats it even more. Let go of the pressure—go on a retreat, practice silence—and it all rushes up, an eruption of fury. The head noise turns dangerous, and secrets you'd rather not know bubble to the surface.

Theologian Thomas Keating calls this the "unloading of the unconscious." This is when old psychic wounds swim to the surface like poisons sweating through the skin. This is when the illusions fall and self-knowledge emerges. Now the spiritual life begins; now the noise is in earnest. Fury, pain, horrible sadness, searing fear, the surety of death, the possibility of absolute failure rise like mares of the night, like fairy pucas, like gibbering trolls. Now comes the true haunting. Now comes the war. All those frets, those worries, those demons you have set aside, the neuroses, the delusions, the night terrors, spring up and face you. Those wars you told yourself you'd deal with tomorrow come brawling back. One demon goes underground and seven return. This is the time when most people run, when cowardice overtakes them. No therapist can make this moment go away; he or she can only bring it on. The retreat master cannot make it go away, either; he is all mind, all teaching, all wisdom. He can only force you back, a sergeant major of the soul. You, the lone human being facing the night, must stick to your tackle and clamor like a champion, a hero with one sword facing the onrushing horde. The horde is yourself; you have made it, given it a horrible life. Sooner or later it will fall on you; better now than later, when you are wholly unprepared. When the horde first arrived, my thumb was tracing circles on the plate. The anger I felt for Annie and Peter and the whole situation had invited them in. The silence I had endured had flung open the door. And they came.

By the time I finished the dishes, the twilight had congealed; the sky had turned the color of an ocean trench, with bioluminescent stars floating in the black. My stomach twisted. The children, chased out of the night by their mother, tumbled into the house, pulling me out of the silence. I stirred, wiping my hands, as they chased one another around the small room, then ran to the kitchen, pulled the ice cream out of the freezer, spooning great gobs into bowls. Within thirteen and one-half seconds, they were fighting over who had more, and who should do the spooning, and why should Tommy have the biggest bowl? Annie stayed on the porch, refusing to mediate. The smoke of her cigarette curled around her head and, moved by the soft breeze coming through the screen, flowed back into the living room. The children screamed. A bowl of ice cream landed on the floor. Annie didn't budge but stared through the screen into the night. I looked at the gob of ice cream on the floor, and at the crushed face of the littlest, whose bowl it had been.

Pick it up, Tommy, I said. You dropped it.

Tommy glanced at it, and then at me, and suddenly wrapped himself in his Uncle Peter's attitude. I don't have to listen to you, he said.

I sighed, took his bowl from him, gave it to his sister, whose eyes widened at the sudden bounty, and sent him out to sit with his mother. He balled his fists, stood up, stared at me with perfect hatred, as only a ten-year-old can, and stomped out to the porch. Annie didn't move, didn't look at him as he sat next to her on the floor. I cleaned up the spill, then stretched out on the other porch lounger, because Annie had taken mine, and read Suzuki until nine. Tommy whined at his mother about the ice cream, but she ignored him, and he pouted. Then he looked at me, considering, stood and politely asked if he could have a bowl of ice cream. I looked up from my book, said sure, and he left for the kitchen. Soon, Tommy returned with a full bowl, sat at the edge of his mother's lounger, spooned it into his mouth, and smiled at me. I smiled back.

Annie lit one more cigarette, a look of ragged defeat passing over her face. She was silent, but her silence was sullen and cold, not like Joe's silence, the silence of attention, the silence of presence. Where Joe's was a living thing, Annie's was not. She hobbled toward despair, like someone newly returned from the front lines. Without speaking, she stood, ignoring Tommy's eyes on her, wandered into the bedroom, and closed the door. Left alone with the children, I pulled a stack of sheets and blankets out of the storage room, shook three blankets onto the floor of the living room, opened a sheet on top of each one, and tossed a pillow onto each bed. The children didn't have toothbrushes with them, so I dug into the storeroom. The place was used for small retreats, and so we kept an emergency store of toiletries there. After a few minutes, I found three unused toothbrushes still in the boxes and handed them out to the kids. I pulled the tube of toothpaste out of the medicine cabinet, squeezed a glob onto each brush, and then said to them, Okay—brush brush brush! They brushed, vigorously if not competently, and I pointed out the three makeshift beds.

Pick one, I said, and they squabbled over which bed was better. I stepped in. You, you, and you, I said to each child and pointed to a bed. They're all the same. The children must have been more tired than they appeared, because seconds after taking off their shoes and settling into the blankets, they were asleep. Sighing, I reclaimed my porch lounger, pulled my sleeping bag up to my chin, and drifted off. My last rational thought before crossing that unseen line into sleep was that there was still no sign of Peter.

The next morning, I awoke with the sun in my eyes. Blinking stupidly, I slumped at the edge of the lounger, my mind blank. Somewhere in my body energy gathered, and somewhere inside my head a clock ticked away the time. I pushed myself upright, swayed once, grabbed the back of the lounger, then sock-hobbled toward the kitchen to feed the Mr. Coffee. The children were still asleep. In the night, they had inched together, blankets and all, until they ended up in a twisted pile in the middle of the room. The Mr. Coffee hissed; it steamed; and when the first wave of coffee dribbled into the pot, I smiled. I thought: coffee, nice coffee, nice, nice coffee. Turning toward the bathroom, I saw Peter, curled up into a fetal position on the floor near the cabin door.

Oh shit! I said aloud. Peter lay there with an empty bottle of altar wine in his hand, and a half-empty bottle on the floor by his head. A smell of old fruit and ammonia rose up from him. He had peed on himself in the night, and his trousers were soaked with urine. I had forgotten about the few bottles of altar wine someone had left in the storeroom, so that visiting priests could say Mass. When the Mr. Coffee had done dribbling, I poured a cup for myself and one for Peter, carried them over, and toed him with my socked foot. He didn't move, didn't make a sound. For a cold instant, I wondered if he had died in the night, if he had choked on his own vomit, or simply ceased breathing from alcohol poisoning.

Peter, get up, I said, trying not to wake the kids. I've got coffee.

No reaction.

Peter, get up! I said, a bit louder this time, and prodded him one more time.

No reaction.

At that moment, Annie walked out of the bedroom, her clothes rumpled and her hair awry. She stumbled to the Mr. Coffee, without looking at me or at anyone else, lit a cigarette, poured herself a cup of coffee, then looked down at Peter.

Peter, godamn it! Get up! she shouted, loud enough to startle me. The kids sat up, and the littlest girl cried. Peter stirred, reached for the half-finished bottle of altar wine. I was quicker, pushing it away from him with my foot, so that the bottle fell over and rolled away toward the bathroom. Peter rolled himself onto his knees and started crawling toward the bottle, but I grabbed it before he could get there.

Damn you, Peter said, still on all fours, still staring at the floor.

Get up, I told him.

He reached blindly for the curtain to claw his way to his feet. Give me that, he said, pointing to the wine bottle.

No, I said, and handed him a cup of coffee instead. He took the coffee from my hand, sniffed it, and dropped it onto the floor, breaking the cup. The coffee pooled around the broken cup like a hot spring, with steam rising from the pond.

Give me the bottle! he said.

No. And I think it's time you went down the road, Peter.

Give me the bottle!

No.

At that, Peter lost his belligerence and got whiny. Annie, he said, Make him give me the bottle. Annie made a face, puffed on her cigarette, and said nothing. Peter shuffled over to Annie, put his arm around her, his voice growing hard again. Make him give it, he said. You know how. At that, he grabbed her breast, and she pushed him away, a look of hatred on her face.

That's it, I said. I set the bottle on the counter, grabbed him by the shirt, and pulled him toward the door. I opened the door and yanked him down the steps. The rocks hurt the bottom of my feet, but I was too angry to notice. Peter tried to pummel me with his fists, but his coordination had gone and his strength was hollow. Even so, he connected once with the side of my face, shutting my eye, so I picked him up and threw him over my shoulder, his urine-soaked crotch a little too close to my face for comfort. I carried him down to the pier, my feet sliding painfully on the slimy pebbles of the beach. At the pier, I carried him to the end and threw him into the cold water. He came up spluttering, cursing.

At least this will clean off your jeans, I told him.

I hate you, man! I hate you! I hate you, man!

I waited patiently until he climbed out of the lake, then followed him up the drive to the road, where he stood shaking. Luckily, it was going to be a warm day, so he would not freeze.

Come see me when you've sobered up, Peter, I said. We'll talk.

He stared at me, hugging himself and shivering. The look of hatred slowly passed from his eyes, and for a short while, the demon fled and he was Peter again. With a look of sadness, he nodded, turned, and hobbled down the road, his boots squishing water as he walked. Standing in my socked feet, I watched him until he turned the corner on the dirt road and disappeared, then walked back to the cabin, feeling the war rage drain from me. When I returned to the cabin, Annie was sitting on the porch lounger, smoking a cigarette and looking at the lake. The broken cup of coffee was still on the floor, so I grabbed a paper towel and sopped up the liquid, while picking up the larger pieces of stoneware with my fingers.

I poured two cups of fresh coffee from the Mr. Coffee and carried one to Annie on the porch. Holding the cup out to her, I looked into her face, and there was a wisp of emotion in her eyes—gratitude? friendship?—and then there was a jerk of fear, and a quick withdrawal. Tentatively, she reached up and took the cup from my hand.

You're welcome, I said. She looked at me, a flash of sorrow, then a quick, shy smile.

I stretched myself onto the opposite lounger and balanced my coffee cup on my chest. The day warmed; a gang of sparrows chattered in the bushes and trees. A boat chugged past on the other side of the lake; just past that, on the highway, a truck downshifted, once, twice; a dog barked in the far distance. A miasma settled around us, a ghostling of Peter's tantrum. A headache started up somewhere at the back of my neck and moved upward, spreading into a wide band around my temples, pressing in. Annie's littlest crawled up beside her mother and tried to snuggle. At first, Annie drew away, pulled into herself, but the girl only snuggled closer until Annie relented, put her arm around her, and with a look of surrender, put her chin on the little girl's head.

What are you going to do now? I said to Annie.

She lit another cigarette, waited a long time, staring at the lake, before she answered. My sister Angela's coming for me sometime, she said.

Today?

She shrugged, puffed on her cigarette.

She knows where you are?

She nodded, puffed again.

Throughout the morning, I read Suzuki, and then Merton, trying to regain the peace I had found the previous afternoon, but it remained just outside my reach. I breathed, but the knot remained; parts of myself were walking down the road with Peter, or standing over him spluttering in the water. The world was too much with me. Instead, I slept, haunted. A face watched me from the dark, a masked face without eyes. A clock struck. Wind blew, and I awakened with a start. Annie and the kids were walking out the door. I walked to the window to see Annie's sister Angela's old Buick sitting in the drive, Angela at the wheel and the engine running. As I stood in the doorway of the cabin, Annie and the kids climbed into the car without saying a word. I waved to them all.

By three that afternoon, I had scrubbed the cabin and returned to the aluminum chair by the dock. A deep sadness filled me. Then fury. Weeping despair. Hatred. Pain. Each stepped forward into the light, replacing the one before, like a stage actor taking bows, the audience applauding wildly, booing and hissing when appropriate, as the actor retreated into the shadows. The horde was inside me again, setting up camp. How could I get control of it, and how could I hold control once I got it? Peter was near bottom; the horde owned him. He had given over a chunk of his soul to service his appetite for alcohol, that glutton of the spirit who would leave him always hungry. Annie was in some ways worse off than Peter; her appetite was for death. Like an acid, it ate at her hope, her desire for life, her love for her children. Thoughts of the children tore my peace entirely. What would happen to Tommy and the girls? Would they grow up to be Peter and Annie? Would they find some other way? I could pray.

Each of us is a little insane, for history makes us so. The eyes look forward; they cannot turn round to see what's inside the head. The only way, the inevitable way, into the spiritual life is through self-knowledge, and because the eyes cannot turn around, the demons march out and show themselves. This is how healing happens. This is how awakening occurs. The more violent the emotion, the greater the healing. Even in a purely secular sense, contemplation is an act of faith—faith that there is an end to the horde, a time of healing after the war. Christian mysticism has two great images for the spiritual life—sex and war. Sex for the intimate bond between self and God. "Eat, friends; drink! Drink freely of love!" says the Song of Solomon (5:1). War for everything else.

Someone asked the Buddha what he and his monks practiced, and he said, We sit, we walk, and we eat. That's it? Doesn't sound like much—not very dramatic. Who's in charge? Who runs the show? Who's in control? Maybe no one. Control is a creature of smoke; the more I grab for it, the more it floats away. I cannot make things happen. I cannot force myself into peace. I live in this moment, mindfully and utterly awake. This takes a measure of not-doing, but how do you not-do? I know how to do, how to throw energy into life, how to set goals, how to make plans, and how to work work work until things get done, but I haven't a single clue how to do nothing. More than that, I fear it. If I did nothing, what would become of me then?

Not-doing is a kind of war, for me the hardest thing of all. No easy methods, no paint-by-the-numbers. It is an art, different for everyone. The retreat master has given me advice, of course. He says: Look, kid, learn to accept. I say: Accept what? He says: Whatever comes. I say: But what if what comes is bad? He says: Accept that, too. Accept everything, good and bad, painful and pleasurable, happy and sad. What comes—is. It is your truth. I say: Yeah, but what if I'm a jackass? He says: Then you're a jackass. Once you know that, you can change it. But as long as it stays buried in there, you'll never change. The truth will set you free, kid, but who says it has to be fun? He's right, of course, and I hate him for it. Most of my life, I have been a circus act. The Great Juggler. For your edification, I shall now juggle twenty-five separate things at the same time! Balls in the air—oohs and ahs, gasps, murmurs of wonder. But what if I had said: For your edification, I shall now do nothing, nothing at all, but I shall do it very well! I shall accept things! Who would pay to see a man accept reality? Where's the entertainment, the thrills, the feats of derring-do? But for people like me, addicted as I am to activity, doing nothing, learning to accept, is so much harder, and to do it well is so very much harder that it goes beyond my ability to wonder. No oohs and ahs, no murmurs of surprise, just a blank stare from an audience who couldn't possibly understand, or see its value. Seems unfair. Accept whatever comes? Maybe I'm just boring.

A Jesuit friend of mine once said that he could never be a monk because he couldn't stand to do all that nothing. Monks, Christian and Buddhist, specialize in doing nothing and in doing it very well. Not that they're lazy—far from it. No one works harder than a monk, East or West. But like my Jesuit friend, when I try to do nothing, I usually end up watching TV, which is just another form of running on automatic. Does this mean that I can't find peace, because I can't guarantee the outcome? The silence is not findable, not exactly. All I can do is sit, walk, and eat, and try to be aware that I am sitting, walking, and eating. For Christians, this is the same thing as finding God in all things, and in all moments. This is the one thing that neither Peter nor Annie could ever accept, because they could never accept their own existence. That way leads to madness. Each person is a little mad—we are sorry, and we are ashamed of ourselves, but well, there it is. Sanity is what people wear on the outside, a new suit of clothes. It's brushed; it's neat; it's color-coordinated. But insanity—*my* insanity—is unique, special, secret, personal, intimate. I am crazy in my own special way. It is what I hold dear, what I secretly love, and yet, what I do not wish to see, what I hate most of all, what enslaves me. After Peter and Annie left that day, I tried to tell myself that I was different, immune, saner than either of *them*, and I succeeded for a while. I believed it because, well, I'm as crazy as the next guy.

That night, I sat in the aluminum chair and watched the stars. I breathed. I visualized myself as a pool of still water. I breathed some more. I prayed. I read psalms—no luck. Two or three minutes of peace, and my brain winched memories from somewhere; memories that played again and again, scratched and popping like old 78s. Silence eluded me. Anger ulcerated me—anger at Peter, anger at Annie, anger at myself, anger at God. Underneath the mask, the mask of my dream, the mask of my public self—the kindly priest, the courtly gentleman—was rage. A killer. A Son of Sam. The horde. If I could only hold out, I told myself, tomorrow would be different.

I awoke early that morning, startled, clawing for air. I glanced at my watch—4:30 A.M. Somewhere in the night, I had dreamed of drums beating and then of hands holding me down in deep water. I tossed the sleeping bag off and made a face at the world. Fifteen nasty impulses pushed at me—I wanted to kick a dog, or pop some kid's balloon, or say something really cutting to some hapless third party. I wanted to do some damage to something, and I didn't care what. Luckily, there wasn't anyone around to beat on, so when the sun came up I decided to chop wood. I love to chop wood when I'm in a bad mood—I get to hit something and it doesn't hit back.

On the shady side of the cabin, tangled in the thick growth, where all the spiders and bugs lived, two dozen unchopped logs hunched against the wall, big pieces of wood itching to be turned into little pieces of wood. I hauled out the first log, and my nose wrinkled at the musty smell of rotting leaves corrupted into a brown ooze. A nest of gray spiders scuttled toward the shadows. I set up the log. *Whack!* That for Peter and Annie. *Whack!* That for parishioners. *Whack!* That for bishops. *Whack!* That for Parish Councils. *Whack!* That for the Knights of Columbus. *Whack!* That for, um . . . that for the bingo. Yes, that for the bingo. *Whack! Whack!* I hate the bingo. *Whack!* That for drunks. *Whack!* That for rotten fathers. *Whack!* That for rotten mothers. *Whack!* That for children with no one to love them. *Whack!* That for babies crushed by rocks. *Whack!* That for those mother's eyes that won't go away. *Whack!* That for the whole bloody world of misery.

Three times, the dull blade bounced off a log and nearly busted my ankle, but I whacked on—pieces flew, kindling accumulated, and my pile of firewood swelled. When it was big enough, I was going to take it inside and one by one throw it in the wood stove and set *fire* to it.

An hour. Enough. I grabbed an armful of wood and carried it up to the cabin door and stopped at the foot of the stairs. I had forgotten to close the door on my way out. Inside, I kicked the door closed and set the wood into the cradle next to the stove, opened the stove door, and stuck four pieces inside. Then I wadded up a piece of newspaper and stuck that under the logs. A box of matches from the goody drawer—I struck one, froze, flame on the match head quivering. Something fluttered overhead.

A bird, I thought, shaking the match out.

I poked into the bedroom, the storeroom, and the bath. Nothing. I assumed I imagined it and knelt beside the wood stove again. Then something fluttered overhead once more.

I stood, ready. What is this? I thought.

It fluttered again, near the screened-in porch. Ouuuw jeez, I said. A bat. A shadow fluttered into the kitchen and clung to the curtains, then fluttered back onto the porch. I walked to the kitchen counter, put my hand on the top, and came up with something white and pasty on my fingers.

Bat shit.

My hair itched as if there was a creature crawling in it. There is something primal, something visceral, about bats. Never mind all the nature shows that tell us how beneficial they are, how they keep us from being up to our elbows in mosquitoes. Never mind the goodness of each creature in its own biological niche. This is all true, but beside the point. This was a *bat*. Think death, disease, and the taint of evil. In the caverns of the psyche, they are creatures of the Evil One, harbingers of bad dreams. They are plague with wings. As if it knew it was being watched, the bat flew back and forth across the living room, taunting me, first to the kitchen, then to the screened-in porch, then back again, wheeling and turning as if it had air brakes, dropping spots of guano on the floor, on the sofa, on the porch lounger, on the kitchen counter. I wanted it gone.

I opened the door and stood aside to see if it would fly out, but it kept to its rounds from the porch to the kitchen and back again unaware. I closed all the interior doors I could find—the bedroom, the storeroom, the bath. Once, miraculously, the bat flew out the door by the kitchen and I rushed to close it, but before I could get there, the rotten little thing flew back in.

Grabbing the broom out of the niche beside the pantry, I started after the bat, sweeping the air in crazy eights. The bat wheeled a few inches ahead of the broom, sliding around it as easily as I would walk by a chair. I grunted and swatted at him harder, if not much faster. If I could herd him to the kitchen and block him, I told myself, I could shoosh him out the door. After ten minutes, I was chasing him around the room, screaming and swatting at empty air, until with one blow, I base-hit one of the living room lamps next to the chesterfield and sent it flying. It crashed, showering the floor with amber glass splinters from the base.

Damn it, damn it, damn it, damn it! I said.

It was all the bat's fault. In the logical part of my head, I reminded myself to take a break, to practice my breathing, to find serenity. I reminded myself that the spiritual life requires a holy indifference to life's troubles, and that I would someday achieve this, someday after I'd strangled that miserable little winged rat with my bare hands. I threw the broom down, just to show him, and stomped out the door. I stomped around the yard, then started up the car. I backed up the drive to the road, then drove on to Squilax, and over the bridge to the highway. Somewhere between Squilax and Chase, I realized that my personal madness was lying just under the surface. I saw my own mad face—mad eyes wide and mad hair awry, raving like poor Eddie Sokalski. Eddie had been my parish's local psychotic, a big man, bigger than me, which was saying something—six-foot-four, three hundred pounds. He had been an ordinary guy, like every other ordinary guy, yearning for the perfect mate, the perfect job, the perfect life. For five years, he worked at the copper mine; the copper poisoned his blood and damaged his brain, leaving him paranoid and schizophrenic. Once a month, he came to see me, raving, and over the years I learned the art of managing his madness while waiting for his mother to arrive with the doctor. Eddie's mother was a slight, elderly woman with a thick Polish accent that reminded me of Maria Ouspenskaya reading pentagrams on the palms of wolfmen.

Eddie's cycle, too, was as predictable as the moon. He stayed on lithium for three weeks, and he would be right as rain until he persuaded himself that he was just fine, that he didn't need that miserable drug, which made him feel dopey. So he'd forget a dose; then he'd forget two doses. At first, it was wonderful, energy pouring through him. He had fifty—a hundred—world-shattering insights every hour, but then they came faster, and turned into voices, and the voices talked faster, like a crowd all rumbling together, and the rumbling got faster, like bees, like static. Then he'd be in my office, shouting, rocking, trying to stop the noise by beating the palms of his hands against his ears.

Even in his most insane moments, Eddie only wanted what we all want—an answer; and even in his most insane moments, Eddie's questions were the same as anyone's: How did I get this way? What's going to happen to me now? Still deeply into my bat disaster, I drove down the highway toward Chase, glancing at my face in the rearview mirror to see if I could see Eddie in my eyes. Once in town, I stopped to see Ian, the mechanic working on Albert's car. As I killed the engine, Ian sauntered out of the garage, wiping his hands on a dirty rag.

Hey there, he said.

I looked around to see if Albert's ancient blue Buick was still there. I see you got Albert out of here, I said.

Ian nodded. That boy can be a pain in the arse. You know that, eh?

You have spoken truly, I said.

Ian looked at me, cocked his head, still wiping his fingers. You look like you've got a problem.

If you call having a bat in your cabin a problem, then I have a problem.

A bat, eh?

A bat. And I've been trying to get rid of it all afternoon.

Ian snickered. Don't tell me. You took a broom to it.

Yes, and it didn't work.

No. I wouldn't suspect it would. Sounds like you've got a problem.

Thanks. I know that.

Got guano all over the cabin, too?

This isn't funny, Ian.

Ian grinned, then snickered again. Yes, it is.

Are you going to help me out, or not?

Sure. I'll help you. You can't use a broom on them. They're too fast.

I figured that out already.

Then get yourself one of them big old coffee cans, eh? And when the bat lights somewhere, stick the can over it and trap it, but don't use your hand, because the thing could be rabid, and if you got yourself bit, it wouldn't be much fun.

Did this coffee can thing work for you?

Ian turned ninety degrees and looked out over the lake while he spoke. Well, no. My cousin Gerry told me about this thing with the can. Worked for him, but it never worked for me. I had this bat in my house once, and I tried the can but the bat got away.

How did you get rid of it?

I didn't. I think it's still in there.

Your house must be a mess.

Oh, it's a dung heap, he said.

I looked at Ian, and he looked back, then dropped his head and quivered, until his laughter broke through.

Thanks a whole bunch, Ian. You've been a big help.

I turned, but Ian came over, put his hand on my shoulder. Wait, wait, wait, he said. I'm sorry; don't go away mad. The coffee can will work, and if it doesn't, try a scoop net.

I nodded. Okay, I said.

At the cabin, I rooted around the trash for a coffee can. I had left the door open while I was in Chase, hoping that the bat would figure it out and fly through, but when I walked back inside, it was still there, flying its circuit. I grabbed the broom, so I would have something to stick over the opening of the can, stood near the center of the room, just off the bat air lane, and waited. I quieted myself, seeking inner silence, seeking oneness, inner peace, Zen and the Art of Bat Hunting. Ten minutes—the bat tired itself out and landed on the drapery behind the chesterfield, near the glass door leading to the screened-in porch. I am not generally good at sneaking, but I did my best, toe first, heel next, moving slowly until I barked my shins against the coffee table in front of the chesterfield and swore. Skirting around it, I leaned over the chesterfield, gently, gently, and caught the bat inside the can. It fluttered, birdlike, squealing almost out of human hearing. I brought the broom up to hold in front of the can, but realized at once that it was too thick, and that I'd have to tilt the can too far to get the broom in front of it. Still holding the can against the drape, I looked around for a piece of cardboard, but there weren't any in sight, only pillows and lampshades. Then I saw it—a Johnny Mathis record album—"Johnny's Greatest Hits," on the side table, on the other side of the chair catty-corner to the chesterfield. I stretched myself, holding onto the can and pawing at the album awkwardly with the broom. It inched toward the edge of the table and fell off. I herded the album toward me but couldn't reach it without bending, so I walked the coffee can down the drapery, sinking onto one knee. I stood, exultant, and the can tilted just enough for the bat to escape.

Damn it, damn it, damn it, damn it! I said, and threw both the can and Johnny Mathis onto the floor.

For the next forty-five minutes, I chased the bat around the living room with the coffee can in hand, waiting for it to light, but the bat never landed more than a few seconds before it flittered off again. Disgusted, I threw the can aside and stomped through the storeroom looking for the scoop net, and found it stuck behind an old pair of skis in the back of the closet. Armed again, I came out of the storeroom and swung the net at the bat, and then swung again, and again. Soon I was chasing the bat around the living room, vaulting over the coffee table and chasing it around the dining room table. The same hunter's blood that drove the woolly mammoths off cliffs, that hunted buffalo on horseback, that tracked caribou over frozen tundra, had emerged, and I was caught in an ancient struggle. A mad laugh bubbled up my throat, and I skirted around the coffee table, leaping finally, smoothly, gracefully, just as my foot caught on the edge of the table, and I sprawled onto the floor, cracking my head against a wooden chair. Momentarily dazed, I turned my head and found a pile of white guano on the floor three inches from my nose. Suddenly, I was cold, efficient. I would have my solution; I would have it.

Standing on unsteady feet, I wobbled to the door and out to the car. A trickle of blood ran down my face near my left eye, and I swiped at it with my hand. I glanced at the smear of red, then wiped it on my pants. At the car, I pulled out my over-and-under shotgun, ripped open the box of shells, and stuffed a handful into my pants pocket. Cracking open the shotgun, I stuck two shells into the chambers, snapped it shut, and stalked back to the house, determined. Inside, the bat was still flying its circuit, and this time, I closed the door with my foot. Empty of feeling, I fired one shot at the bat, missing, and ripped a hole in the drywall next to the bathroom door. Moving to the center of the room, I fired another shot, missing, and shattered the kitchen window, splintering the sash underneath. The bat was still alive. I cracked open the shotgun and popped out the spent shells, stuck in two more, and fired once again. This time, the bat was clinging to the porch screen, and when I fired, it flapped once, twice, and tumbled to the floor, twitching. The madness was gone.

I looked at the shotgun in my hands, and at the bat flopping helplessly on the floor of the screened-in porch, at the hole in the screen, now an open door for flies, coming and going, at the window above the sink, at the shattered glass scattered on the floor, at the chunks of wood blasted off the sash, at the hole in the drywall.

I looked down at the shotgun again. Eddie.

Oh shit, I said. No one could ever know.

Eight

SITTING ON THE FRONT steps, my back to the wounded bat, the shotgun astride my knees. Not wanting to think, or know, or see. Cracking open the shotgun, teasing the spent shells out of the barrel, balancing them hot on my hand, feeling the empty weight of them, smelling the sharpness of the gunpowder, rubbing at the residue smudge on my thumb and fingers. A tree full of sparrows on the other side of the car flutters. The birds tattle on each other and hop back and forth on the branches. A single airplane flies overhead, its engine grinding as it climbs out of Kamloops east over the Rockies. That's a long climb, I think vaguely.

The shotgun feels cold and smooth and hard on the tops of my thighs, and I absentmindedly trace the intricate carvings on the stock with my thumb, picturing the bat crawling helplessly, like a man in search of water, a few feet from the shattered glass of the window and the chunks of wood blown off the sash. My sanity seems a fragile thing, too easily upended, and a chill shivers me from inside a hollow peace. The horde had subsided like an old tide, melted into the sea, leaving behind only a sniveling boy of eleven. That was it? That was the horde? This boy? Ignore the man behind the curtain, the Wizard said. How embarrassing—the fears, the night terrors, the rage masking nothing more than a self-centered, confused child. The retreat master said to me: Look, kid, of course it's embarrassing—embarrassment is life, ever since you were caught naked in the Garden of Eden. You stand firm and you'll see—the horde, they're just ghosts. Ghosts you created, inventions of your mind.

Thus the great hunt ended, and I had broken every rule. You hunt moose and elk to survive, to feed the kids, to triumph over nature, to transcend mortality, and to drink beer. But I had tried to kill the bat because I was too pissed off not to, and turned my will over to this child rampant, who took me where I didn't want to go. The memory of those fifteen long seconds, when I had forgotten myself, my adulthood, my civilization, rattled me. I turned to face the water. The concrete steps felt cool on my backside, and the lake felt smooth on my eyes. The stillness of the evening soaked through my skin, through the muscles, and into the bones. This happened of itself, not in my control—my insides stilled, and I became a pond of deep water, unstirred by wind, unrippled, smooth. For the moment, the child slept.

Standing the shotgun against the cabin steps, I climbed to my feet and slouched into the living room. The bat was still wriggling on the floor. My rage had transmogrified into fellow feeling, into compassion for bats everywhere. I searched the storeroom for a shoebox, then grabbed the ash shovel from the fireplace kit and scooped up the bat, setting it carefully inside the box. The bat wriggled to the side of the box and curled up there, one wing splayed out, spotted with blood. Kneeling beside the box, I wadded up old newspapers and put them inside to make the little creature more comfortable, like packing a fragile glass sculpture. Then I scooped up the box and started toward the car. Looking down, I saw that the bat had died. I prodded it gently to be sure. Sadness twisted me. As a boy, I had captured a horned toad and built a home for it in a shoebox, but my father told me to let it go, because I didn't know how to care for it and that it would die. I couldn't do that, because in the fashion of ten-year-old boys, I loved the horned toad too much. Then it died—starved to death. I showed the box to my father, who said: Now it's dead, and its little life will never come back. Not ever. Prodding the bat, I was ten years old again, flushing with the primal shame of Adam, caught in the act. I mourned the loss of that little life, the life that would never come back. Not ever.

Something broke inside me at that moment, a shift as if an icebound river had cracked and began to flow freely. Some people, like Peter, are addicted to alcohol; some, like Annie, to their own wounded states of mind. Eddie was addicted to the rush, to his own insanity. Everyone I knew was addicted to something: some to food, some to power, some to fear. I was addicted to brain noise, to the action, to the itch to be doing something, if not outside, then inside my head, chasing answers to unanswerable questions, probing, demanding, insisting on solutions to life that in the end are only made of dreams. I was addicted to control—not over other people, but over myself, and over the future. I was addicted to the fear that if I ever lost control, I would go crazy. But there it had happened—like Eddie, I had lost it.

After spiraling out from a particularly manic episode in which he'd menaced the bishop, Eddie Sokalski shot himself in the head. I presided at his funeral, marshaling out the Knights of Columbus and the Ladies Sodality to pack the church. Eddie's mother held a white handkerchief to her nose and quivered with grief, while the Knights in their plumed hats and swords loaded the casket into the hearse. She said to me, as if to make an argument:

My Addie! My poor Addie! He was crazy in his brain. And they did that to him. My poor Addie! He was a good boy, you know that? A good boy!

I put my hand around her shoulder and said yes, I knew that. At the cemetery, high up on a hill overlooking the town, I sprinkled holy water on the casket and prayed a poetic benediction.

May the angels lead you into paradise.
May the martyrs come to welcome you,
and lead you to Abraham's side,

where Lazarus is poor no longer,
and every tear will be wiped away.
May you have everlasting rest.

As we were walking back to the limousines, one of the Knights, a righteous protector of orthodoxy, leaned toward me and whispered: I'm not sure he should be buried in consecrated ground, Father. He was a suicide, after all.

I stared death rays at him until he backed away. Eddie was a good boy, I told him, and meant it. Eddie, I knew, was no suicide. The noise had killed him.

I took the box with the dead bat outside behind the cabin, and digging a shallow hole, wrapped the bat in a paper towel, and buried it. In the cabin, I cut a piece of cardboard and taped it over the broken window. After rummaging in the storeroom for a roll of leftover screen to wire over the hole I had blasted into the porch screen, I fixed the damage and then hobbled to the aluminum chair to watch the afternoon pearl into evening. I yearned to move, to take the boat onto the lake, to drive into town, but fought against it, allowing every impulse to wash over me as it came.

The lake water rippled softly pink in the last moments of the day. A mockingbird landed on the shoreline near my feet, hopped back and forth, turning its head, pecking in the rough sand, and hopped again. I watched absently for a minute, my thoughts flitting with the bird, and then the bird flew away. As night strengthened, the nattering of the sparrows thinned, faded into single voices, a call, a warble, and bit by bit, into silence. Twenty feet offshore, a bat flitted, a bare shadow in the thinning light, wheeling in the air, hunting mosquitoes. I breathed, the rhythm of my breathing sober and methodical, like the tolling of a bell; with each breath, the madness washed further out of me and the child faded into the past. Like the birds, my mind stilled a bit at a time—a half-finished sentence, an impulse, a quick desire to be about something—and I accepted each one, and let it go, and watched it pass, indifferent, as it floated away and pinched into black, like the last message of the day from a television station going off the air. I kept breathing, my thoughts gathered into a bunch, pressed into a single awareness of air rushing up my nose, past my ears, down my throat to my lungs, filling all the way, tight into my gut, filling all of myself with air, sipping it, holding it inside, and then letting it out again, softly, smoothly, without force or hurry. The retreat master said: That's it, kid, that's it. This is how it's done. After the war—peace. I was breathing, and I knew that I was breathing. I was sitting, and I knew that I was sitting. The awareness drifted higher, and I floated off toward sleep but held myself there, hovering inside, yet oddly feeling as if my body no longer ended with my skin, but kept going out with each breath of air—into the shore, into the lake, into the trees. The stillness deepened from a puddle to a pool, to a pond, to a lake, to an ocean. The real person, unnamed and unnameable, the self who blends into God, was there in that deep place, and neither the boy full of anger nor the man full of shame could touch him. The noise of my life, the retreat master said, was merely an old habit.

The next morning, I awoke on the porch, the sun in my eyes. In my direct line of sight was the hole I had blasted into the screen the day before, and the flies circling above. I staggered to my feet, slipped on my tennis shoes, and fed the Mr. Coffee. My skin told me that the day would be bright and soft, dry with the promise of wind later in the afternoon, the kind of weather that made people in fire season look nervously at the surrounding hills. I carried my coffee down to the aluminum chair. The rhythmic sloshing of the water against the shore bathed me, and for fifteen whole minutes, I sipped black coffee and thought of nothing at all. Birds squabbled in the bushes. Filmy clouds striped the blue overhead; a three-pound bumblebee hovered over my lap, inspecting me for pollen, and then flew off. For the first time in weeks, God seemed everywhere; not the God of the storm cloud, not the God who killed babies, not the God of the black hole, but the God of the silence, the God who maintains everything in the pleasure of existence. Pseudo-Dionysius, a sixth-century Syrian monk, said that no name could ever be adequate to God; that no quality, no act, could ever contain God. Could we say that God is good? Yes, but no. Could we say that God is love? Yes, but no. This is not a problem with God, but a problem with language, that poor starveling, too weak of bone to harrow out the Mystery. But what is so special about God, then? I thought, sipping black coffee. The same thing could be said about a morning like *this!*

The morning was a sacrament, a communion, and everything in the world ate bread and wine. Consume the sky, consume the water, consume every sound. A high-pitched motor approached from around the point, and a ski boat appeared, and a young woman with streaming yellow hair waved at me, smiling. An osprey soared overhead, and dove toward the water, pulling up at the last minute, a real flyer, reaching out with a single talon and snagging a fish. The hills across the lake were still dark green in the shadows, lightening to that special kind of green that can hurt your eyes if you stare at it too long, with patches of dark fir running up and down, sheltering deep places under the thick growth where mule deer lie up in the day, coyotes and foxes build dens, and bear wander through on bear business, snuffling for wild blueberries.

In the middle of this, Ian's old aluminum bass boat pushed around the clump of trees on the point, following the skier. He waved at me and cut his engine, turned in toward shore, and tied up at the pier.

What you doing out here, Constable?

Brought you some beer.

It's a little early, wouldn't you say?

I would, but there are rules. Beer is what you're supposed to bring when you visit.

I understand. But since it is still early, you can put the beer in the fridge. I have coffee made, but you'll have to get it yourself.

Ian walked past, whistling some old Mountie thing. I listened as the door opened behind me, and while he was inside I told myself that it didn't matter what he thought, or what any of them thought. I was just fine.

I heard Ian's whistle, heard him rummaging around under the porch for the other aluminum chair, heard him pull it open and try to bend it back into shape, heard him grunt, and then he appeared, sat on the other aluminum chair, his coffee sloshing onto his pants. This second chair was bent in exactly the same way the first was, so the two of us, side by side, leaned against the bend like sailors. Ian glanced at me, but said nothing about what he had seen inside.

I heard about what happened to you in town.

What town, and what did you hear?

In Kamloops. The baby.

Oh, I said. That.

Tough.

Yes. It was tough. How'd you hear about it?

Ian looked at me with mock surprise. You know I hear everything sooner or later.

I'm sorry, I said. I don't know what came over me.

How'd your bat turn out?

I got it.

Ian nodded, a hint of a smile on his face. He looked at the water and sipped his coffee. I never told you why I retired from the RCMP, did I?

I shook my head.

I was up north. Used to work in the city, and then got transferred to the Okanagan, but even there, I felt like I was running in circles. So my wife and I packed up and headed north. The kids were old enough, and we wanted to find the quiet life, but nothing changed. I was like you, always having to do something, think about something, fret over something. All I wanted to do was think about my cases. I reorganized my filing system six times, and then did it again six more times. I went off to workshops, just to get away, and was worse when I got back. I think I nearly drove my wife to drink. She left me for a while; it was in the middle of a hard winter, and I was alone for the first time in twenty years. Spring came, and she wasn't coming back, she needed more time. That's when the bat got into my house. I tried the broom. I tried the can. I tried the net.

So what did you do?

Grinning, Ian reached his fingers into his shirt pocket and dropped two spent shotgun shells into my hand.

III
The Third Circle of Silence
NO SELF

SUSCIPE OF ST. IGNATIUS

Translated from the Latin by J. Connor

Receive into your hands, O Lord,
my whole liberty.
Accept my memory, my awareness, and all my will.
Everything I have you have lavished upon me,
and I restore it to you,
to be directed according to your will alone.
Give me only your love, and only your grace.
Then, I am rich enough!
I ask for nothing more.

IGNATIUS OF LOYOLA

Nine

I CRASHED INTO ADOLESCENCE on a Saturday afternoon, standing in the hall bathroom of our house in Los Angeles, looking in the mirror, combing my hair. First, I tried shaving, but there wasn't anything to shave, so I dabbed a pearl of Brylcreem onto my head, smeared it around, worked the hair into place, shaping and petting, with each follicle combed into position, leaving one perfect curl to drop down to my eyebrow. For the next twenty minutes, I practiced sneering at the mirror—a tight lip curl, Elvis-style, the once and future King—turning sideways, sticking a hip out, and slouching into it, liquid and dangerous.

At thirteen, I dreamed not of girls—at least not directly—but of cars. There I am in my new Corvette, stopped at a light, the engine rumbling like a captured dragon. A car full of girls pulls up, and I stare straight ahead, aware that they are watching me, then slowly, oh so slowly, I turn my head, cocking it lazily to one side, the perfect curl dropping down, my head bobbing to inaudible music, and with one eyebrow raised for invitation, I sneer at them. And they are devastated.

Then my sister walks into the bathroom and giggles, and I am ashamed of myself.

God said: "Who told you that you were naked? You have eaten, then, of the tree of which I had forbidden you to eat!" (Gen. 3:11) And the man was ashamed. The rest is history.

The problem is not with being naked. The problem is with knowing that you are naked, or with knowing that nakedness is a problem. Everything else in the universe except me and my fellow humans is naked. The mountains are naked, the lakes are naked, the birds are naked, the deer are naked, the bears are naked, all the trees are naked, standing forth as they are, without a lie, without a hint of shame. The day is naked, the wind is naked, the clouds are naked, the earth itself—all naked. Except me. I have on jockey shorts, the kind with the yellow-and-blue stripes in the waistband, olive cotton work pants, argyle socks my sister gave me as a joke, Alpine boots, an L. L. Bean flannel shirt, and a light cotton jacket. I alone am dressed. This wasn't always so. When I was two, I ran around in the joyful altogether, in gleeful escape, and if I was quick or lucky, I slipped by my mother's capturing arms and ran naked and giggling down the street to the neighbors' to dance naked on their lawn until my mother scooped me up and ruined all the fun. You should be ashamed of yourself, running around naked like that, she said to me, and laughed.

When I was nine, my allowance ran out and the one comic book—Detective Comic # 46—I wanted above all others hit the shelves at Hal's Drug Store. Hal wasn't going to open up a line of credit just for my comic books, so I stole it, lifted it from the shelf, stuck it under my jacket when he was busy on the phone. It was that easy, and no one had seen. For the first week, I read it once, then again, and again, exulting in sweet larceny, in the confectionery smell of theft. Of course, I never told anyone, not even my buds. Only chumps blab. So why did Hal look at me so oddly the next time I stopped in with my mother? Had he noticed the comic bulge as I had walked out the door? Had my mother noticed it when I came in? That evening, my mother gave me the same look, and chewed her lower lip, as if she could see a long prison sentence unrolling before me. For the next two weeks, whenever my father called me, I was certain he knew. I felt naked. He had to know! My mother had to know, too! All my brothers and sisters—somehow they knew. My teachers, my friends, my neighbors. Everyone was *looking* at me with that knowing smile, understanding, piercing the veil, pressing on the dark and inky spot that lay buried in my soul. Eventually, I confessed, brought the comic to my mother, and sank onto the footstool beside her in shame.

I knew something was going on, she said, and frowned at me. Looking back on it, I don't think she had a clue, but she had to say it, just to sound omniscient. Wait until your father gets home, she said. And I waited.

That night, my father marched me down to Hal, and I slid the comic book onto the counter in front of him. My father prodded me in the back, and I told Hal that I had stolen it, and that I was very, very sorry, and that I would make it up to him. Everyone seemed immensely tall. Hal looked down at me, my father looked down at me, the lady at the counter buying an enema kit looked down at me. I was standing naked in a forest of disapproval.

That's all right, Hal said. I'll hold onto this comic book until you get your next allowance. Then you can come buy it.

I nodded, feeling relieved, but on the way home my father said, Mr. Breinstein was very kind to you. After all, you should be ashamed of yourself. And I was.

Thomas Merton says that a false self shadows each one of us. It is a creature, a golem, a monster. I build it from my imagination and my desire; like a necromancer, I spend my days breathing life into it. The creature embodies all my hopes for power and glory, the man I yearn to see in the mirror, the once and future King, the man I want to be even if I am not. It is constructed partly of dreams, partly of expectations, and partly of shame. I give it power every time I go into the world thinking myself grand. Every time I put on a show, I shoot electricity at it, and give it more life. "All sin," Merton says, "starts from the assumption that my false self, the self that exists only in my own egocentric desires, is the fundamental reality to which everything else in the universe is ordered." All my airs, my vainglory, my pomposity go into making it live. My real self is buried deeper, until the only way out of the labyrinth is intensive therapy—a patient counselor and the willingness to face the truth. I feel guilt when I see how much this golem runs my life. I feel shame when anyone else sees it. Hold yourself lightly, the retreat master says. Like the air in your palm, kid, barely feel it. The self you clutch so tightly isn't real, but only air, a pretense, a play of light and shadow. The real you is deep, the long forgotten you, the child who runs naked and free, who plays and enjoys. The real you is the one you have unremembered, trying to be so adult, trying to be in charge.

This false self turns on the idea that who I am is not enough. Somehow I must stand out. I have to be visible, obvious; I have to be noteworthy, memorable. The worst thing in the world is to be mediocre, white bread, insipid, unsalted. The false self is amoral and thinks nothing of consequences as long as it survives and becomes noteworthy. Whether that notoriety comes from being a hero or a villain is a matter of personal taste. When I was in school, I was the detention king of Our Lady of Grace Elementary. I earned detentions for every little thing to the point that the sisters wearied of giving them to me. I became heroic to my peers, a celebrity bad boy. Later, I became a priest, surprising them all; my bad-boy youth was soon forgotten, and I was famous because I was good. My life as a soap opera—same story, same plot, different week. The false self lives; the false self breathes, and soon, I forget that the false self is only a mask, a self-creation. I mistake it for me and struggle to keep it alive. I tie myself into knots, and tell myself I am only doing what I have to do. I have no choice—go on or be ashamed of myself.

When Ian returned the next day in his ancient Dodge pickup, we drove to Salmon Arm to buy building supplies to hide the bat damage, and I spent the day itchy, alert to the slightest hint of judgment. Sitting with my hands in my lap, I half caught Ian's loose chatter about the next local disaster, about whose kid had been arrested, about the spot fire in the hills, and about rumors of the firebug who'd been running wild in the mountains. The best Ian's truck could do on the highway was a little over forty-five, because most of the energy the engine put out went into making the doors rattle. One after another, cars pulled up behind us and sat on our tail for a few miles. I turned the passenger side mirror to watch the faces of the people behind, and one after another, male or female, they went through the same pattern of expression. First, a look of forced patience and resignation, which slowly froze to a mask, tightened lips, eyes focused like lasers on the back of Ian's head; then the mask broke, the hands flew up in irritation, then the pointing, palm up—where do those idiots think *they're* going? Ian ignored them, chugging along, chattering about recent traffic accidents and dropping police appropriations and just what did the government think the RCMP was going to do with criminals, give them a tongue-lashing?

I felt naked. I felt judgment around me like a magnetic force field holding me in place. Helicopters circled overhead pointing floodlights at me, circling, circling, unspeaking, watching. I listened to Ian's talk for subtle references to the bat. So he had done the same thing years before. So he didn't seem to care one way or another. The fact that he knew I had gone mad for fifteen seconds was enough.

In school, the sisters reckoned that guilt was a good substitute for religious awe and told us that God took note of everything we did, describing in exquisite detail how our guardian angels standing beside us broke down weeping at our most subatomic infraction of the rules. We all imagined God looking through the roof of the building, jotting notes on a yellow pad with a number 2 pencil, and then shaking his head at our guardian angels, who were keening with grief. Because I had held the record for the most detentions at the school, I felt a constant need to rush out and confess. I must have done something wrong, I reasoned, or I wouldn't be feeling this way. Over the years, I realized that the eyes watching me were not really God's, or my mother's, or the sisters. The eyes were mine, the judgment mine, the disgust mine, and my great fear was that I might let something slip, a chance word, an unguarded moment, and someone would do a little math, figure out who I really was, and feel the same way.

As Ian talked, I tended the silence inside me like a new fire. The silence was there, underneath the shame and fear of discovery, warm and comforting though I knew it was incomplete. There was still the all-seeing Eye—my Eye—me watching me watching me watching me—and every level of self-watching carried an unspoken, implied commentary, a commentary that I would not let materialize into words, but that I nonetheless understood in full.

Meanwhile, the Big Shuswap Lake slid into view. It was twenty-five miles long, fed from ice melt off the Rockies. I had explored much of its western end for good fishing holes, but the eastern end, near Salmon Arm, was far enough off that my little boat couldn't make it there and back again inside of a day. Salmon Arm is a fair-sized town curving around the end of the lake, reluctantly spreading back farther into the hills. The hardware store was a mom-and-pop affair, up on top of a knoll overlooking the lake, a perfect view if people hadn't built tall houses just below so they could peek over the tall houses below them. Inside, the store was garage door white, with most things racked or stacked or hung, while the rest was piled into the corners collecting dust. Overhead, country music played softly from a speaker. A fellow with a salt-

and-pepper beard and an I.D. badge that said "Wilson" over his breast pocket came up to us and smiled.

What can I do for you? he said.

We've got to make some repairs on a cabin, Ian said.

Well, you've come to the right place, Wilson said. We've got everything you could want, from lumber to concrete.

Ian held out a list. You have all this? he said. If you don't, there's a True Value in Kamloops.

Wilson snapped the paper out of Ian's hand. Let's have a go at that list, he said. One piece of drywall; a can of premixed spackle; two gallons of eggshell white wall paint; a window, twenty inches by twenty-five inches; ten feet of two-by-sixes, for the sash I take it; seventy-five feet of porch screen. Wilson looked up at me and then at Ian. Old cabin? he said.

Party, Ian said, glancing at me.

Must have been quite a party, Wilson said. A beaut.

There it was. I could feel my face coloring. Ian glanced at me, bent away, coughed once, twice, three times. My face heated like a laundry press. Wilson looked at Ian.

He said, You all right?

Ian nodded, held up his hand, the wait sign. Something in my throat, he said, half choking.

You want some water?

Ian shook his head no.

You smoke? Wilson said.

Ian nodded.

That'll do her, Wilson said, nodding toward the back room. My wife made me quit two years ago. Said she wouldn't pay the funeral expenses. He ducked his head, tapped the list with his finger, silently mouthing the items, and disappeared into a room at the back of the store.

Control yourself, I hissed at Ian.

Don't be so sensitive, he said, still coughing. At least I didn't tell him what the repairs were really for. My face heated like a nuclear reactor. I wanted to go sit in the truck. I wanted to sit under the truck. I didn't want anyone to see the violence skulking inside me.

Wilson returned and, seeing us waiting for him, he ducked his head and smiled salesmanlike. The three of us bundled all the items to the front register and I watched horrified as the tally grew to $175. On a priest's salary, that was a great deal of money. For fifteen seconds of violence, I was out nearly two weeks' pay.

In ancient Ireland, the poet Cairbre of the Tuatha Dé Danaan once satirized in rhyme the local king Bres for his meager hospitality, and Bres putrefied of shame. Shame is a killing disease, a curse, a voodoo doll with pins. A man could die from shame. When I was two years old, "shame" meant that my mother didn't want me to have any more fun. When I was nine years old, "shame" meant that I had done something wrong, and they all knew about it. When I was thirteen years old, "shame" meant that something was wrong with me, I didn't know what, but *they* did. People were not only looking, but thinking, judging. Could they *all* be wrong? Could the whole world, judging me as it was, be wrong? The easier thing to believe, quite logically really, was that there was something fearfully wrong—with me. What that wrongness was, I wasn't sure, but it was there, because I felt it. I felt the distortion like a hump unseen, and I was Quasimodo, a half-made man. I was in danger of making shame the condition of my life, feeling forever that first moment standing in the locker room butt naked, covering myself with a towel the size of a Kleenex. That moment had spread out thinly across my adolescence, as if God had appeared in the locker room and turned to me and said, Who told you that you were naked?

Hold yourself lightly, the retreat master said. Be willing to find humor in yourself. The false self exists only as long as you are watching, and vanishes as soon as you forget, in joy, to do so. The habit of watching, however, is an old one. In adolescence, my false self made a bid for control, and I wanted to be more than I was, and every day the definition of that *more* changed. I was forever on the road in my rumbling Corvette, on the highway to someplace wonderful, where the people would see me, desire me, fear me. And I would sneer at them, and they would be devastated, and there would be no shame because no one would ever realize that I was standing behind a cardboard cutout. But this sweet dream was fragile—a shadow dance. Shame was its natural reward; shame was its final truth. Shame for the false self is like the terror you feel before God, knowing that your own existence is questionable. It was in adolescence, then, that shame became a part of me, sewed itself into my DNA, and wrapped itself around my veins and arteries.

The putrefaction of Bres came from inside him. Cairbre's poem would have had no effect if Bres had not been willing in some twisted way to agree with it. Shame is mind noise, an endlessly critical nasty voice keyed to the all-seeing Eye that watches and judges. Me watching me watching me watching me, and it never ends until I give it up, and I can never give it up until I find freedom in silence. From adolescence on I have stood in the house of mirrors watching my own reflection copied a thousand times through a thousand trick mirrors, and all of them false. Sometimes I am a dwarf, sometimes a giant; sometimes I am too fat, sometimes I am bare bones; sometimes my nose hangs down to my feet, sometimes my ears are three feet wide. And the voice whispers: *This* is why you're wrong; no, wait, *this* is why you're wrong; no, no, wait, *this here* is why you're wrong. I have seen myself a thousand times, judged myself a thousand times, condemned myself a thousand times, and a thousand times executed myself. As Mark Twain said, "Man is the only animal that blushes, or has need to."

Look, kid, the retreat master says, the only way out of shame is to be indifferent to the past and the future, and to hold lightly all the facts of your life: whether you are rich or poor, tall or short, beautiful or ugly; whether you achieve your dreams or fail at all you attempt; whether you are honored or dishonored, famous or obscure, powerful or powerless. Hold lightly to health, to well-being, even to life. For Christians, Jews, and Muslims, this is possible because all things live and exist in God. It is possible for Buddhists because enlightenment reveals the true nature of life. In all cases, kid, hold yourself lightly. You are created in the likeness of God, kid, and the truth of your existence is greater than anything you could grasp by force of will. There is meaning and purpose and dignity in that truth, woven in before you were born. But you have to be worthy of it; the greater the dignity, the greater the struggle. If you want to live, kid, be willing to die. If you clutch at yourself, that self will be false, and you will eventually slip away. Paradoxically, if you hold yourself lightly, you will remain. You will no longer need to be prettier, richer, smarter than others. You will be as pretty or as rich or as smart as you are, and that is good enough. Other people's opinions will fade, pale things, without power to wound or mend. When you are healthy, you will remain yourself. When you are sick, you will remain yourself. When you are dying, you will remain yourself. You will lose nothing. At all times, living and dying, the core truth of you will abide.

This is why you have to keep your sense of humor, kid. Mirth! Mirth is the answer. There it is, our common humanity in the twists of our illusions. Pierce the veil, reveal the deceptions, the self-serving arguments, the biases, the prejudices. Reveal that you are like everyone else in this world because you have the audacity to think yourself better. Is there nothing funnier? A knee-slapper! A side-splitter! Laugh, and then remember to dance, to play, to sing in the shower, to live.

I have an imaginary ancestor I once invented to explain my genetic makeup. His name is Osric Axewielder, and he is six feet tall, muscle-bound, with fair skin, and he blushes. I would buy stock tomorrow in any genetic research company that could come up with a cure for blushing. It is the curse of my life. When embarrassed, my skin heats up and my face reddens, which triggers a salivary response in everyone around me, so that they instinctively blurt out: Oh look! You're blushing! Girls think it's cute. I don't. When I die and face my ancestors in the Great Beyond, I intend to have words with old Osric. I am certain that I was blushing, Osric-like, all the way back to Ian's truck, all the way out of Salmon Arm, all the way back to the cabin.

If only I hadn't been watching myself so intently all along, Ian's little jokes wouldn't have rubbed so. I wanted to stop watching but I wasn't sure how. Whenever I tried, the only way I could be sure that I had was to check, and the only way I could check was to look and see, but the only way to look and see was to keep watching. When I realized that I hadn't let go, then I had one more failure, one more black mark I could put in the book. For Ian it was just good fun. As we turned onto the road to Squilax, Ian pointed to a gold Chevrolet Impala that was driving past, and said: Hey, wasn't that your bishop? My intestines twisted. Had the bishop been to the cabin and seen the damage? I just spent $175 trying to cover up the evidence, but had he been there before me and seen it all for himself? I was doomed. It was Hal the shopkeeper and my father and the lady buying the enema kit all over, only this time I had passed puberty, and I knew what he might possibly think—not that I had *done* something wrong, but that I *was* something wrong.

It couldn't have been, I said.

Yeah, I think it was, Ian said.

It couldn't have been. What's he doing out here now? I thought he was in Toronto, I said. I peered at the car, which had turned onto the highway, off in the distance. That's not his car, I said. His car is lighter.

That was him, Ian said. I know that car.

We both watched the car disappear into the distance. Ian looked back at me, his grin not so wide. Oh, you're in deep doggy-doo now, he said.

Maybe I could lie, I thought. Maybe I could make up a good story, a whopper, like maybe vandals sacked the place, or maybe I caught a bear inside the house, or maybe I had a nightmare and woke up with a sledgehammer in my hand. I had to keep the bishop from finding out the truth, that I was capable of violence, capable of shooting an innocent bat with a shotgun. That I, Dr. Jekyll, was also Mr. Hyde.

When Ian and I returned to the cabin, there was a note from my neighbor, Dr. Bennett, on the door. The note said the bishop had stopped by his place and was going to come to see me, but he ran out of time and asked the good doctor to offer his apologies.

You lucky bugger, Ian said over my shoulder.

I leaned against the kitchen counter and read the note two times. All the while the universe expanded, and then collapsed. The irony was so awful I had to choke down a mad giggle. I escape by a twitch of circumstance; the universe slides on and I skate by a monumental embarrassment, an embarrassment that never would have happened if I hadn't been out here in the first place, and I never would have been out here in the first place if an innocent baby hadn't been crushed to death by a falling stone. Ian looked at me, puzzled, and I looked away. How could I tell him; how could I put it into words? How could I trust a world so full of mad twists?

There was a time in my life when I trusted because I didn't understand. I trusted my parents, my teachers, my friends and neighbors because they were bigger than me and knew what to do. I was a child, and I was innocent. That is what innocence means—to trust without knowing, to trust what other people say because we trust *them*. But then I became a priest, and every day I faced life and death, disease and madness. Every day I faced life as it is, wondrous and awful, all at once. One baby dies, another miraculously survives. Not miracles for everyone, and not death for everyone, but a terrible winnowing, and nobody knows why.

Knowing all of this, trust is the most difficult thing in the world, and yet the only thing. Life is here, and I am in it, and the Mystery is here, and I do not understand it. The rest is up to me. I can live my life if I choose, knowing that somehow the universe works out. It is not perfect, but it gets by. By trusting, I affirm life while recognizing death. I slip the bonds of my false self, and hold lightly to my defenses. By trusting, I can face life as it is and let go of a fear that threatens to drown me.

Trust is a choice. It is something I do because I want to be the kind of man who trusts. There is no joy in life otherwise. To do this, I know I must abandon my old habits, let go of my old fears, face life and death as they are, and like the Buddha recognize the *fact* of suffering. I must give up *me*—at least the me that I thought was me—so that I can make room for the true self buried and long forgotten. No words, no mind, no *self.* I am a man hanging from a cliff by his toenails, a man who cannot climb up and cannot climb down, and the only answer is to learn to fly.

I set aside the note, and Ian and I got to work. In two hours, we had repaired the porch screen. Ian was a much better carpenter than I was, so I let him work on the window and sash, while I cut a patch out of the drywall and opened up the hole in the wall to fit the patch.

We had the cabin put back together by the end of the day. While I was painting the wall, I heard a low whistle and turned. Albert stood in the middle of the room, shaking his head. I ignored him. The sun fell gold and crimson yellow on the surrounding hillsides, and I opened up the trunk of my car to get out my personal six-pack of beer, stuck the cans in the freezer section of the fridge to get them cold in a hurry. Twenty minutes later, the three of us sat on the screened-in porch, drank beer, and watched the zipping world gradually come to rest.

Ten

Fire purifies the forest as silence purifies the soul. We were sitting on the dock when the radio man said that another burn had started five miles from the old one, and that a front was pushing in with a whole new set of winds. Ian listened, lips tight, then told us suddenly he was needed elsewhere. When he had gone, I returned to the floating dock to watch the ruby fire glow on the hills, hands in pockets. I was captivated by the night, purified by the silence, my insides burning free. It was the blue time of the evening, and swallows snagged mosquitoes from the air at ramjet speeds. Cabin lights along the lake popped on like new stars igniting. Loons warbled from the middle of the water, while aspen and hemlock glimmered purple silver with the last light. God poured through each tree, each blade of grass, a secret fire quivering the world. The evening seemed more lucid, sharper than usual, and I felt like a man putting on glasses. My eyesight cleared, my hearing intensified. I breathed in the thousand vegetable odors of the forest, the copper tang of the lake, the sweet sharp smell of pine, and felt more aware that night than I had ever felt in my life. Ten o'clock, with stars scintillating overhead, I carried my sleeping bag down to the dock, and as I drifted toward sleep, the mountains glowed silver in my dreams—in the dream, there was a distant hum of airplanes.

By the next morning, the earlier fire was still burning away to the east, pouring smoke into the sky, fouling the air like a rusty steel mill. A forest rots or it burns—it burns slowly, or it burns fast. Dead branches, dead logs, dead needles, tangled undergrowth building up over the years, clutter the forest floor, breaking down over hundreds of years, choking out new life. A forest fire burns away the dross. Most fires start as ground fires—lightning strikes, runaway campfires. A moist duff covers the ground in thick shade where the sun never dries the soil, and in those places, the fire smolders. But if it crowns, rises to the tops of the trees, then it can become a monster. Since 1950, there has been an average of 624 fires each year in the area covered by the Kamloops Fire Centre. Once a decade or so, a fire will cover tens of thousands of acres, take months to control, will hop as far as a mile in a high wind, killing anything in its way. You can be standing on a hillside, thinking you are safe upwind, and the wind will shift and the fire will get away from you and you will die, as quickly as that.

When a fire crowns, there is a muscular power to it. It creates its own wind, drawing oxygen to itself, swaggering, blowing itself over vaster and vaster territories, with embers like dandelion seeds on a breeze. In *Young Men and Fire,* Norman MacLean describes how a fire

> is even more unpredictable if there isn't much of a wind to begin with, because a big crown fire can make its own wind. The hot, lighter air rises, the cold, heavier air rushes down to replace it in what is called a "convection effect," and soon a great "fire whirl" is started and fills the air with burning cones and branches which drop in advance of the main fire like the Fourth of July and start spot fires. The separate spot fires soon burn together, and life is trapped between the main fire coming from behind the new line of fire now burning back toward it.

If the space between the spot fires and the main fire heats up above the point of ignition, and if a fresh wind blows new oxygen into the space, there might be a "blowup," and the fire will explode out of control. I hadn't heard whether the new fire had crowned, but it had already spread over dozens of acres by midmorning. Whether it was an offspring of the first fire, or the brain fever of some lunatic with a can of gasoline, we never knew.

The silence that morning had set fire to my insides, burning away the deadwood, clearing room for new life. I sat in the aluminum chair on the floating dock and watched the column of smoke slowly curl over the trees, without a book, without a thought in my head, without words—just coffee. The silence burned away illusions, false selves, and old dreams, leaving a heightened awareness that drew me closer to the world. I breathed, and with each breath, the fire burned hotter. In the fourth century Abbot Lot once came to visit Abbot Joseph in the Nile desert and said to him: I keep my little rule as best I can. I fast, keep silence, meditate, and as much as it is possible for me, I try to keep thoughts out of my head. What else can I do? Abbot Joseph stood and stretched out his hands to the sky. His fingers burst into ten flames like lamps, and the old abbot said: Why not be turned utterly into fire?

Existence is a flame. It is not an accident that fire symbolizes the spiritual life. What is the universe but a 12-billion-year-old flame? I once saw a Van Gogh painting at the National Gallery in Washington of a field and a green bush, with brush strokes like green flames twisting and rising, and was shocked by the truth of it. What is a tree but a slow-burning fire? What is an animal but a fire that burns faster? The Spirit is likened to flame, either to flame or to wind, the feeder of flame. The god of the Zoroastrians was Ahura Mazda, the Unquenchable Fire. The God of the Hebrews, whose name cannot be spoken, was a pillar of cloud in the daytime and a pillar of fire at night. When the Holy Spirit descended on the Apostles, tiny flames danced above their heads. Even when I am not filled with the Holy Spirit, my body is a fire, oxidizing on the spot, a heat engine balanced on the blade of too much heat or too little, the balance held in check by the structures of my cells. I suffer when the fire burns too low. Mornings on the lake my fingers and toes ache with cold, even in summer. Frostbite had made them more sensitive than they should have been. Oddly, when winter is deep, the tips of my fingers feel as if they are on fire, so all summer, I chop wood so I can spend the winter at the fireplace, hands out warm near the flames.

But fire is more than this. It is purification; it is the cleansing of the soul. This is the idea behind Purgatory, the fire that cleanses the heart even as it does a forest. My life is littered with emotional detritus, and the only answer is to burn it away, to throw gasoline on it like a lunatic firebug, strike a match into flame and toss it on. In knowing God, you have to become a human torch. There is nothing more painful, nothing more like fire, than learning to hold oneself lightly. You can no longer be the center of your life. You can no longer live in your dreams. As long as you keep yourself, your petty needs and wants, at the core of things, you will manufacture a terrible illusion. Mortification is the way out. Purification is the emetic. An act of courage and emotional maturity takes your little vain self and puts it over *there*, making room at the center for that which cannot be named. Conversion is a change in appetite, small in the beginning then gradually permeating the whole self.

In Buddhism, enlightenment is the only way out of suffering. Suffering comes from desire, from that swirling, wriggling need, that biting, that chewing, that constant eating. Burn away desire, and you see into the depths. Purification is freedom. Purification is new life—I am purified; I grow in conversion; I lose a taste for myself, and gain a taste for God and the world and the secret fire that burns at its heart. I fall in love with everything that is, everything that, as the poet and Jesuit priest Gerard Manley Hopkins said, "flames out, like shining from shook foil." Only this way can I see God's face.

Monasticism, East and West, intensifies life by simplifying life, which is the chief reason why both traditions praise poverty and asceticism. The more stimulation I have, the more demands I have on my attention, the more diffuse I get. When I go on retreat, I go to a place where there are no phones, where no one can beep me, where there is no TV, and even the radio reception is poor. I am addicted to these things. By living simply, by paring stimulation down to a nub, the things, the people, the activities I love swell to fill my life entirely. Simple food, simple clothing, a simple schedule increase the level of appreciation. Simplicity intensifies each moment by making room for the fullness of living.

By six o'clock that morning, the sun was rising, and I wanted peanut butter. Peanut butter on toast. I rifled through the kitchen cabinet, where I had stashed a small jar of extra chunky, a secret treat. I knew that Albert was a peanut butter hound like me, so I hid it amid an array of tomato soup cans, certain of my cleverness, but apparently this was not enough. The jar was gone. He must have found it in the night and carried it off to his room. I pictured him eating my peanut butter with a soup spoon—I'd seen him do it before—until it was all gone, and then hiding the empty jar under his bed. And that smirk on his face! I growled in the back of my throat. Police action. SWAT teams. I wanted to barge into the room, demand the peanut butter, or at least the evidence, and send him packing!

I leaned on the counter, furious, and the retreat master, inconvenient as ever, was suddenly there in my head. Now, kid! he says. Now is the time for purification! This is it! Not two weeks from now, not a year from now. Now! If you don't do it now, kid, when you're mad about peanut butter, you'll never do it. And if not, you'd be all talk, kid. Let go of the peanut butter. I say: Let go? How can you ask me to suffer like that? It was my peanut butter. And if I have to suffer, can't it at least be more dramatic? What's the point of suffering if it can't be dramatic?

Don't I at least get beheaded? Tortured? Even a little? If I'm gong to be purified, I'll at least want to make a good story out of it. He says: Real life is about peanut butter, kid. And purification is about real life. Ordinary life, tedious life. Bear it with equanimity. You can't choose your mortification, kid; life presents it to you every day. It's dealing with life, and that's what makes it mortification. I say: You're so smug. Why do you know so much? He says: I'm Jiminy Cricket, kid, except I can't sing.

Mystery permeates the world and each thing in the world through their common existence. This is far from what I was taught in Catholic School, where the Mysteries of Faith were those theological formulas that defied logic. That Mary was conceived without sin, that Jesus was God and Man, that God is both Three and One—these are Mysteries of Faith. The Mystery I awoke to that morning has no category, no formula. It folds into everything like yeast into dough, and dances just beyond the edge of language. It is the vestibule of enlightenment, the alpha and omega of science. To know that you do not know is the still point of wisdom. To know that *you* do not know is the still point of self-understanding.

The door to wisdom is silence, a silence that embraces ignorance. In silence, the Mystery breaks over me. Of all human actions, only silence is the most inexhaustible. As Thoreau wrote in his journal: "I have been breaking silence these twenty-three years and have hardly made a rent in it. Silence has no end; speech is but the beginning of it." At each stage, silence deepens and expands, teaching me something new. First, with Joe's help, I learned that the habit of silence is an art that can be acquired, like painting or music, and that the life of a contemplative butts up against the life of a poet. For all my theological education, or maybe because of it, this came as a shock. Next, I learned that silence implies peace, and that all the noise in my head was a kind of addiction that sooner or later, like any other madness, could kill. The head noise had to go. Then, diving deeper still, I glimpsed something more, like a flash of water through a stand of trees, a deep place in the silence, more profound than any I had yet encountered, where my own self dissipates to reveal something hidden. This new something would take my entire life to plumb. From that time on, I felt like a man rappelling into a cave too deep to see the bottom. I had awakened to the living mystery in everything, including me. I could not watch myself into existence any longer; I had to accept my own existence as a Mystery wrapped in the Mystery of God. As a Zen retreat master once told me: "First there is the mountain; then there is no mountain; then there is the mountain again." You accept the mountain's existence with innocence. The mountain is just there. Then you realize that there is really no mountain at all—it is at bottom a Mystery, its independent existence an illusion, part of the illusion that is the world. Then you see that not only is the mountain a Mystery, but so is everything else, even me, and so the mountain is on the same footing as everything else. Then you see the mountain again.

I was in college when I first learned how to fight fires with a chain saw. The advantage of a college education. It was a summer job, working for a company that tested safety limits on explosives. The job was a ten-year-old boy's dream—blowing stuff up! We staged our shots in a canyon on the lee side of an extinct volcano just west of the Rio Grande, near Socorro, far enough out of town to protect the citizens, but not far enough away to cause trouble. One morning, just after sunrise, we shot .50 caliber machine-gun bullets at a solid-fuel rocket, one at a time. Twenty of us, young men and women, hid in the blockhouse seventy-five yards away, sitting on the concrete floor, fingers in our ears, while the boss plugged the cables into the board, set the timer, and watched on the closed-circuit television. A countdown—the gun fired. Nothing happened. No explosion. Relieved and disappointed, we breathed, stirred, all at once. Everyone stood, joked and prodded each other like kids out of the blockhouse and halfway to the rocket, when the woman in front of me said "*Jeeezus*! That thing's on fire!" A thin stream of smoke curled out of the bottom of the rocket, which rested on a concrete pad, chained to the ground with foot-long steel stakes. We stood, frozen, halfway between death and safety, waiting to see if the damned thing would explode. Instead, the smoke thickened, and fire roared out of the tail section. The rocket lifted off the concrete pad, pulling the stakes out of the ground. The fire was red, yellow, green, incandescent and sun-bright, beautiful. It arced over us and landed half a mile down the road on the hillside, a hundred feet from where a second crew was raking shrapnel out of the ground. This time the rocket did explode. Miraculously, no one was hurt. The second crew stood and watched, mouths open, as the rocket curved toward them, hit the ground, and turned into fire. But all too quickly, fire licked the side of the hill, flaming greasewood and mesquite, igniting piñon trees up and down the canyon.

Pumper trucks from World War II clanked toward us from the main building, but the fire was growing too fast. The boss appeared in a camouflaged pickup and handed out chain saws and safety goggles to us; we were still standing agape on the path halfway between the blockhouse and the concrete pad. Two flatbed trucks followed the boss, a cloud of dust billowing like a dirty fog, and we clambered into the beds, our chain saws at our feet. About a half a mile downwind from the fire, the boss shouted: String out and cut brush in a strip a hundred feet across, then pull the brush to the side of the cut opposite the fire. Starve it, he said. Starve the fire! I put the goggles on, fingered the chain saw, something I had never held in my hand before, pulled the cord. The chain saw popped, sputtered, and died. The boss walked over, took the saw from me, pushed the primer bulb three times, pulled the cord, and the chain saw buzzed to life, spewing white smoke out the side. He turned it off, handed it back to me.

Have you used one of these before? he said.

No, sir! I said, shouting over the chain saws and the fire.

Well, don't cut your foot off! he said.

Ian drove up to the cabin in his old Dodge. He slammed the rattling truck door with a hollow metal sound and leaned against the cabin. I peeked over the side of the truck bed and saw seven chain saws, several new, the rest beat to hell.

The new fire, he said. A front's coming in. They expect the wind to shift sometime this afternoon, and they want a new firebreak. I volunteered us.

You and me? I said. Or Albert, too?

Albert, too.

Albert, too, what? Albert said from behind me. And hey, where's the coffee? He was barefoot, held an empty cup in his hand, and still had the look of morning stupidity on his face.

Help save the forest, Albert, I said. You know, like Smokey the Bear?

Ian talked on as if he hadn't heard us. There's a spot upwind of the fire, he said, where the trees are thin. We can start the cut there. It's out of harm's way now, but if the wind shifts, it could get dangerous. We'll have to get out of there fast.

You love this stuff, don't you? Albert said to Ian.

Ian opened up the truck door, pulled out a packet of envelopes, and threw them to me. Your mail, he said, and walked past me into the cabin. Standing with the coffee cup still in my hand, I leafed through the envelopes—a late bill from PetroCan, an advertisement for Yes! Even more credit!, an announcement from the bishop, and a fancy stationery envelope with muted roses on the front and no return address. Intrigued, I finger-ripped the last one open and pulled out a matching piece of stationery paper.

Dear Father,

Thank you for staying with us so long that day. I am sorry if I wasn't very pleasant. The doctor has me on a medication that has helped alot, and I only hope that it can keep me from having to go into hospital. He says that I am depressed, and I suppose I am, but I guess that is to be expected. My husband sends his best. He is very sorry because he wasn't pleasant that day, either. We've decided not to go back to our house for a while. Our families are here and we are happy to have our parents around. This has been hard on my husband's father. We hope you are well, and we hope that you will come see us soon.

All best wishes

P.S. Please pray for my baby.

Holding the letter in one hand, I collapsed onto the cabin steps as a tide of fellow feeling engulfed my chin and tightened my throat, and I felt the pain of my helplessness rise again. The tragic life of one woman had crossed paths with mine, and in the crossing sent ripples into every part of the world. All the years I studied theology had not prepared me for this letter, which had opened questions like wounds with no answers, no balm for healing. Here in this note, I realized, was the Kingdom of God. Here in the life of this woman was the pearl of great price. The Spirit blows where it will. Who was I to know that it would blow me here? I backhanded a tear off my cheek and reread the letter, the flourishing round script trying to be elegant, the lines meandering over the page, the blotches of ink dabbed unsuccessfully from the paper.

A letter from a *girl*, eh? Albert said from behind me. I turned to face him, found him leering, and held his eyes. He backed away, embarrassed.

When I was twelve, the burden of being twelve sometimes pressed on me, and when it did, I set out walking down suburban streets, twisting up into the empty hills behind our home, to a place we called Mecca Valley, no one knew why. Hiding among the California holly trees, I meandered along old trails looking for snakes and horned toads, snacking on peanut butter sandwiches and bags of Fritos. Now and then I wandered across an invisible line and crossed into 20th Century Fox's back lot, where a guard in a pickup truck eventually sent me home. By late afternoon, I dragged into suburbia again, to find my father sitting in his car at the trailhead, reading a book, waiting for me. He said nothing but opened the door and I climbed in. Sooner or later, whatever kid thing that was bothering me would bubble out, because it always did. I had come to the lake for the same reasons, wandering, seeking purification, seeking to burn away the duff and see things clearly. I couldn't have realized at twelve what a pattern I was setting for my life. On the screened-in porch, or on the floating dock, or on the boat, I was still twelve, wandering through the holly trees, working things out.

In the fifth century, Irish monks left their homes on *peregrinatio*—a journey, going out into foreign places—looking for isolated islands. This was an Irish version of the sacred journey, the holy wayfaring, the pilgrimage, where the traveler wanders about looking for the center of the world, the holy place where God once spoke to mere humans. These ancient pilgrims traveled as an outward sign of the interior journey, the climb up Mount Sinai, where the inner landscape burns free of the undergrowth of everyday life. Every place was holy for them, every harbor sacred, every island a God-filled place to live a life of penance and prayer. They remembered the journeys of Saint Brendan, often sailing without a destination in mind, setting themselves adrift, feeling the hand of God in the winds and the currents. The Spirit blows where it will. And so they came to Wales and Cornwall, to western Scotland and to the Faeroe Islands. Some are said to have reached Iceland. Some are said to have reached America.

What could have driven these men to travel the oceans looking for silence? To cast the burden of themselves upon the waters, the selves they had made and reinforced with dreams of glory. To cast themselves upon the waters that they might find themselves. This is the great paradox, the paradox I have never been able to solve, hard as I try, even now. To find myself, I must be willing to kill myself, that manufactured self that so often feels like the real me. I have to let go of all my self-checking. Am I still here? Am I still good? But I can only do that once I've come to some deeper self-understanding. But how can I come to know myself if I don't watch myself? Too, too much me—how can I find my way out of the labyrinth? And so I wander still through Mecca Valley, trying to work things out, hoping Dad will be there at the end.

Albert took the passenger side of the truck, and I jumped into the truck bed next to the chain saws. Ian backed the truck up the drive, narrowly missing a tree and then my car. We drove past Squilax and on up the dirt road toward Scotch Creek, weaving around the hills by the big lake. Sunlight warmed my face, morning air cooled me. We shot around the bends in the road, bouncing into potholes, until we pulled to an open space under the trees. Two more pickups were there, with a small crowd of people, mostly young men, a few in their forties, and two young women in jeans and flannel shirts, their hair tied up in kerchiefs. I jumped out of the back of the truck, nodded to people, while Ian shook hands with an RCMP fellow in a uniform. A police car squatted white on the other side of the trees. After a few minutes, Ian returned and started hauling out chain saws. He gave me one of the new ones and I hefted it.

Borg, I said out loud. Well made. Good balance. Inside, however, I was thinking it was cool because it was brand new and it was yellow.

Do you know how to use one of those things? Ian said.

I think so, I said.

Just don't cut your toes off, Ian said, and walked away.

One of the Desert Fathers, Abba Macarius, was living in Egypt and came on a thief packing the abba's belongings onto a mule. Pretending to be a stranger, he helped the man finish loading the animal and peacefully sent him on his way, saying, "We brought nothing into the world with us, and we take nothing out of the world when we are done. The Lord has given as he wished. Blessed be the name of the Lord." Odd to have thought of that story as I stood at the trailhead with Ian and Albert, the fire boss, and a handful of college kids. Ahead of me was fire, and a part of me was afraid. Why didn't Macarius care whether the man stole his property? Was he so holy he didn't need clothes? Isn't it right to care about theft? Should we hate the good things of life? Wasn't this carrying purification a bit too far?

In the seminary, I read Tolstoy and afterward secretly suspected that I should never again eat desserts. I read the Desert Fathers and thought that I should never again have a full night's sleep. I once tried praying all night, and instead of being filled with the Holy Spirit the next day, I was grumpy and irritable. All my life I had heard about saints who practiced extraordinary feats of self-immolation, and I couldn't stay up one night without crabbing.

The point of purification is not suffering. Suffering is sometimes its by-product, but not its meaning. Anyone who sets out to live a life of suffering for its own sake is not doing this for spiritual reasons. Purification, or mortification—the art of dying—is a scrimmage on holding yourself lightly, field practice, teaching you to hold your own soul in an open hand. The wind blows away the chaff, leaving the true self behind. This is what spiritual writers, East and West, call nonattachment. It doesn't mean that I look down on the world, or possess an inhuman detachment from the lives of others. It doesn't mean that I don't care—rather the opposite. It means I should have more passion, rather than less; more commitment to others, rather than less; but the passion, the commitment, needs to be directed at the proper target. When you are awake, at each moment, beauty reveals itself. Photographers spend their lives looking for it—a dune lit by the evening sun, a bluebird in a tree, a mountain with its head in the clouds. In each moment, there is something there, something indefinable, a name that cannot be spoken. For those with the right attention, for those who can see, God pours through every moment, every blade of grass, every flash of a human eye. But to see this, you have to hold yourself lightly, because if you're too attached to your fears, your anger, your shame, then all you can see is yourself. The universe jitterbugs past, with all the presence of God manifest but without purification, while you sit in the corner whining about your life.

The truth is that I cannot hold onto anything—loved or hated—any more than I can hold onto a breath of air once inhaled. I can't hold onto anything without falling into the trance of the illusory self. The aim of the spiritual life is freedom, and to be free, I purify myself from what Thomas More referred to as "this bothersome thing I call myself." I purify old grudges, ancient lusts gone to ground, false idealism, twisting desires. I release old insults, bless those who have hurt me, release illusory loves and even more illusory hates. I learn to hold all these things in an open hand, and to do good whenever possible—to answer a curse with a blessing, a rejection with understanding. I learn to hold no attachments, to love nothing and no one to the point that I would possess them, to hate nothing and no one to the point that I would destroy them. I grow closer to the world, to my true self, to God if I let the rhythms of life happen as they were meant to happen.

Freedom spawns pain even as it spawns truth. The reward is great, a joy surpassing all pleasure, but I could not know this was so until the first time I felt it, and even then I soon forgot afterward until the next time. One moment I remember was on a late spring day the year after I was ordained. I was crushed by the loneliness of parish life, the hard-heartedness of sinners, including myself, the joylessness of so many believers, the messiness of adult life. I drove to the airport, rented a small Cessna, and tried to fly my troubles away. I climbed through scattered clouds at six thousand feet, east toward the Rockies, through puffball clouds that parted, insubstantial, as I approached. The mountains climbed higher as I flew farther east, the sunlight blanketing the yellow hills and the green green mountains, darkened here and there by patches of shadow. Far below me was a friend of mine at the flying club, a woman named Adele, in her old Stearman doing rolls and Immelmann turns, happy as a seagull, and I smiled. The grind of the engine, the puffball clouds, the blanket of sunlight, and all the day was marvelous. I found it impossible to think of myself for more than half a second without getting lost in the sky and smiling again. The landscape below me was golden, and I knew that something unspeakable was hidden there in everything, beyond happiness, beyond sadness. The joy that I had felt seeing the comet emerged, and I realized that God was there, in the clouds, in the land, in the sunlight, in Adele doing lazy figure eights over Big Shuswap Lake.

The fire boss led us up a narrow trail, a cut in the forest climbing up the high side of the mountain spur, and zigzagged in and out of canyons where streams ran in wet years. The needles crunched underfoot, as if to prove the danger, and though there was little or no wind at the time of the morning, the heat swelled, and we sweated most of the way up. Ian, who was considerably older than the rest of us, sometimes fell back, so I dropped behind and walked with him, but though his face reddened he kept the pace the rest of the way. Personally, I was nearly dead by the time we reached the top, and I didn't care who knew. If I have to suffer, everybody is at least going to know about it. Now and then, we trudged out of a streambed and up the side of a hill, and a column of dirty white smoke cleared the trees to the east. A helicopter arced overhead, dangling a bucket of fire retardant on a cable. It disappeared over the hill, was gone for a few long minutes, and then came whopping back toward Kamloops to pick up a second load.

We arrived at the site by ten o'clock, and the sun beat on the back of my neck as the trail opened into the glade, the remains of an abandoned logging operation. Jack pine stands nibbled at the edge of the open area, while the glade was knee high with hemlock, jack pine, and spruce, mixed in with a scattering of blueberry and salmonberry hugging the ground.

All right, the fire boss said. Here we are. I want you to cut a break about a hundred feet across from this point up, following the line of the hill. The fire we're fighting is a bit more than half a mile east on the other side of this hill, past that dry creek, and up the other side. If you don't know how this is done, I want you to cut this scrub underfoot and haul it to the side away from the fire. About half of you have chain saws; the other half are on drag detail. Pile up the brush on the other side. We should have some D9 bulldozers up here to finish the job sometime late this afternoon. We'd have one of them here now, but they're all busy on other jobs. If the wind shifts, as we suspect it might, I want you all to forget what you're doing and get the hell out of here. You are not professionals. You are volunteers. Helpers. Don't pretend that you're firefighters. You are not. Just get out, and get out as fast as you can. Is that clear? Ian here—the fire boss pointed to Ian—is in charge. Do what he tells you to do. Is that clear?

We nodded like those little dolls in the back windows of cars, and I was sure that not one of us was feeling delusions of fire-fighting grandeur. If the fire came, we would be gone. The boss waved at us, turned, and started back down the trail. I felt like I wanted to follow him. Instead, Albert and I climbed the rest of the way up the hill to get a good look at the fire, and after we had stumbled to the top, we noticed that half the group had followed us. Down the hill and up the hill, the fire burned away on the other side. A line of white smoke poured into the air from the other side of the crest. I wondered how far down that far side of the hill the fire was; then, near the top, a single lick of flame cleared the hilltop, reddening the sky. Another lick farther down, and then another. In five minutes time, flames appeared up and down the hill. We stood frozen, eyes fixed on the monster.

Eleven

IDLENESS IS THE ENEMY of the soul, says the *Rule of Saint Benedict.* No idleness that day. It would be a long, hard day of labor in the hot sun. One by one we left the crest of the hill and wandered down to the glade, picking spots on the ground, forming a line that followed the crest. I found myself fifty feet downhill from one of the two college women, who set her goggles over her eyes, smiled and shot me a little finger wave, pulled on her chain saw, and started cutting. My chain saw, though, was finicky and needed cussing before it would start. Pull after pull, cuss after cuss, I primed it, adjusted the choke, once, twice, pulled once, twice, and suddenly it exploded into life, and I set to work.

Admittedly, my body does not like work. It doesn't mind hiking, running, playing ball, or paddling a canoe, but it hates *work.* For the first half hour of cutting brush, my legs hurt, my back hurt, my neck hurt, my arms hurt, my ears hurt, my eyes hurt. I stumbled, and I wondered how I was going to make it through the day, and Hey, isn't it time for lunch yet? and Jeez, I'd like a drink of water. I had no rhythm and no balance, and with every cut I made, the chain saw came closer to amputating a toe. My own brain worked against me. I lurched through the underbrush, swearing, nearly falling twice, cutting one tree and then staggering on to the next. I felt as if I was moving from tree to tree in a cold-medicine fog. With each step, grasshoppers clacked into the air from the dry brush, clattered off a few feet, and then disappeared back into the grass. Birds picked them out of the air. Eventually, I came to a fifteen-foot spruce, the biggest one around, knelt to start cutting, when a sparrow burst out of the upper branches. A nest was woven up high, with the heads of baby sparrows popping up over the side. I'll leave this one alone, I thought, and moved onto the next one. A team of three college kids without chain saws appeared around me and hauled the tree carcasses downhill to the other end of the firebreak, and the space around me opened.

My high school gym coach was also my first Zen teacher, though he didn't mean to be. Crespi High had just put in a brand-new track and field, and Coach meant us to gather all the benefit from it we could. Every day, he lined us up like marine recruits and marched up and down the line, taking our measure. Somewhere along the tour, he stopped, picked out some hapless guy, and asked him: How many laps do *you* think is fair? The hapless guy would look at his shoes, shuffle, and say: Gee, Coach, I don't know. Fifteen? And then Coach would double it. Once, we tried lowballing him—two laps, three—but then he raised it to the fourth power. Coach taught math on the side. The first three or four laps were hell. My brain churned and my legs hurt—the more my brain churned, the more my legs hurt. Sometime after the fourth lap, however, I awakened—the brain noise had become repetitious and boring. I was actually boring myself, so in desperation, I turned off my brain. By the next lap, my legs had loosened, the knots in my back had smoothed, my breathing had deepened, and my body was moving with a simple, steady rhythm that ate up the laps. The last four, I felt only the movement of step after step, breath after breath, floating from footfall to footfall. The closer I was to the movements of my body, the easier my body moved. The less I thought about finishing the run, the faster the run got done.

This is self-awareness without self-consciousness. There is always a note of criticism in self-consciousness—you didn't do *that* very well—criticism that binds you, throws you back on yourself, separates one part of you—the critic—from the rest of you. You stand back from yourself, your own bad coach, clucking over stumbles, *tsk*ing over graceless movements. Self-awareness has no such critic. It isn't like the self-watching you have done all your life, which is at the heart of self-consciousness. When you are aware of yourself, simply aware, you see without judgment, you watch without criticism. This takes purification, which means that the first four laps are necessary. With the critic silent, every part of the soul pulls into the body, fused, without opposition. You don't stand off, grumpy, arms folded, finding fault. You see and accept, because it doesn't matter whether you do it well or not; it only matters that you find joy in the doing. All bodily movement—running, raking leaves, even cutting brush with a chain saw—has a beauty to it, a dancelike joy in the movement, a pleasure in the breathing. Learning that is so is hard, but only because the task itself is simple. The first thing you have to do is silence the head noise. You slide into the moment of awareness; you let the judgment, the critique, and the impatience go. There is a rhythm to the work, an economy of motion, even a pleasure in the warmth of the day. All you have to do is forget the past, forget the future, and abide in your own body, as I had to on that mountain glade on a hot summer afternoon, cutting brush.

Annie Dillard in her book *Pilgrim at Tinker Creek* said that the door into that ineffable experience of the transcendent present opens from eternity, but it opens into this moment, this particular instant of time. Time is funny. One way, it is a succession of ticks, a metronome clicking the world into the past. Another way, it is an endless now in a changing world. One way, time is breakable into bits; another way, time is slippery smooth. The closer I get to now, to this moment, the closer I get to eternity. Time is objective, to be sure—things are born, things die, things pass from the world. But it is also quite subjective—the passing of time, fast or slow, stretches like a rubber band. In his *Confessions,* Saint Augustine denied the existence of both past and future, and said there was only a now, mixed with a bit of memory and a pinch of imagination. Past and future are inventions of the human mind, he said. The world passes away and we remember how it was; the world is born and we predict how it will be. Yet memory and imagination work in the present, which stretches and shrinks according to our perceptions of past and future. They are part of that wider struggle I wage against myself, and against the belief that my pleasure and my pain are more important than they are, just because they are mine, against the belief that I am a self separate from the world that gave me birth. This struggle is the heart of Purgatory, the holy warfare, the battle between the angels and the spirits of death. One of the Desert Mothers, Amma Syncletica, said: "In the beginning, there is struggle and a lot of work for those who come near to God. But after that, there is indescribable joy. It is just like building a fire: at first it's smoky and your eyes water, but later you get the desired result. Thus we ought to light this divine fire in ourselves with tears and effort."

In an hour's time, I had cut a swath through the underbrush, fifty feet wide and twenty feet deep. The morning slowly turned into afternoon. A single bead of sweat worked in stages down my back to the belt line. Sweat soaked through my T-shirt from the pits down both sides, above the breastbone, and just above the gut, forming dark patches that threatened to pool into one giant sweat stain from neck to groin. Under the baseball cap, my hair had soaked together into a single clump, and my whole body smelled like copper. Up and down the line, chain saws growled like cartoon dogs, and every half an hour or so, I surfaced from my work, from the motion of my hands and feet, to watch how the glade had become a sunny meadow. Tiny yellow butterflies meandered between wildflowers, never lighting, seemingly oblivious to the racket, doing what butterflies do. Bluebirds, woodpeckers, sapsuckers, and sparrows careened between the trees. A shadow passed through the glade; an iron cloud had moved under the sun, big enough to darken the world. A line of somber cumulus, the front they had been worrying about, circled in from the southeast. The air seemed heavier than it did, thicker and more difficult to breathe; the sweat coated my skin, slippery and sour. Suddenly, Ian was there, touching my shoulder; I killed the chain saw. The haulers were running behind the cutters, so we had to stop for a minute and help the college kids haul brush. I set my chain saw down in the base camp, where the trail to the pickups entered the glade, and met with Ian halfway up the crest. For the next half hour, we hauled cut trees and underbrush and threw them on the pile growing on the downhill side of the firebreak. Sometime in there, the fire boss sauntered into the glade, looked at our work, and nodded. It wasn't very pretty, he said, but it would do. Good enough, I thought. We weren't firefighters, we weren't loggers. We didn't know the fine points, but we could hack and haul with the best of them.

The front's starting to come in, he said to us after we had gathered around. The wind could shift sometime soon. If it does, Ian, I want them out of here, no matter what. No heroes.

Ian said sure.

The fire boss looked at us, nodded approval again, and then said: We really do appreciate your help. I couldn't send my regular crews out to do this job. As you can imagine, they're pretty busy. But this firebreak will help if the wind shifts. Keep working hard as long as you can. I'll send some people with refreshments. Then he smiled grimly at us, turned, and disappeared down the trail.

Let's get back to work, Ian said. Can't sit here all day.

Albert sidled up to me and eyeballed Ian. A little bit of power goes a long way, eh? he said.

Well, I said, Ian's a white man. What can you expect?

Albert pursed his lips in thought, as if I had said something profound. You're right there, brother, he said.

There is an intimacy to a life of self-awareness, a flowing together of all your disparate parts into one. Saint Augustine thought that God was more intimate to each of us than we are to ourselves, and that if we only looked inside our own souls, there under the tangle and the brambles of false selves, we would find God, in the simple place where Love exists simply. The deeper we go inside, the more we blend with God. For a Christian, the practice of mindfulness is a practice of presence. When I can be present to my own actions, when I can become aware without self-consciousness, I can become intimate with the God who is already intimate with me.

Connection spreads outward like waves on a pond. The mystical tradition, East and West, points to the connection. Each living thing resonates with each other living thing, like tuning forks ringing harmonies. Francis of Assisi, perceived the mystical connection between himself and everything that existed—rocks, trees, birds, silkworms, butterflies, flowers, planets. And in this unity, the substance is the presence of God. According to Psalm 19:

The heavens proclaim the glory of God
And the firmament shows forth the work of his hands.
Day unto day takes up the story
and night unto night makes known the message.

No speech, no word, no voice is heard
yet their span extends through all the earth,
their words to the utmost bounds of the world.

We worked until three in the afternoon, when four young men with backpacks appeared hauling a tall aluminum jug between them. Ian called a break and we limped over. The aluminum jug was full of sweet iced tea. The backpacks carried boxes of baloney and cheese sandwiches, bags of airline peanuts, and mealy apples. We lined up like veterans at chow, dirty, weary beyond standing, eyes glazing, heads hanging, noses and necks and forearms red as salmon steaks, the dust and the sweat of the day mixing to a fine paste on faces, hands, arms. I was happy to see that the college kids were as exhausted as I was. The young woman who had worked the section uphill from me collapsed onto the ground a few feet from where I was sitting, her back against a fallen log, her head drooping into her lap. She opened the baloney sandwich with her thumb, grunted, and set the plate beside her in the grass, too tired to eat. Albert slouched over and sat on the other side of the young woman, inspected his baloney sandwich, grunted, and stuffed one end into his mouth.

Albert, he said to the young woman, putting his hand out.

Beth, she said, taking his hand.

That fellow over there is Father, Albert said, pointing to me.

Beth looked at me, puzzled. You a minister or something?

Naw, Albert said. That's his name. His dad thought it was funny.

Beth looked at Albert, incredulous, then at me.

Don't listen to him, I said. He just got out of the State Institution. He's okay as long as he stays on his medication.

You're having fun with me, aren't you? Beth said.

No, I said. I'm having fun with Albert.

Her mouth tightened. She was obviously too tired to put up with this.

Actually, I'm a Catholic priest, I said.

Her eyes widened. Oh, she said, as if I had told her I was the king of the elves. I dated a Catholic once, she said.

Well, then, you know everything there is to know.

He was a jerk, she said.

Oh, I said, and went back to my sandwich.

A few minutes later, Ian appeared, just as tired as the rest of us, and sat on the log.

Iced tea, he said contemptuously.

What would you rather have? I asked, feeling like a straight man.

Beer, he said.

And you an ex-lawman, Albert said, primly.

Wouldn't you rather have a beer right now? Ian said, ignoring Albert entirely.

If I had a beer right now, I'd never get up again, I said. There's some question whether I will anyway. I'd be flat on my back, asleep, mouth open, snoring, flies buzzing in and out. Beth looked up from her lap, grinned at the image.

I tore open my bag of peanuts. Albert and Beth looked up and sniffed the air. A shift in the wind. The four of us stood and looked around the firebreak. One at a time, the rest of the crew did the same. Ian, Beth, and I limped as fast as we could up the hill to check on the fire. The rest of the crowd followed us, and soon the whole group stood at the top of the hill watching the smoke curl in our direction. A hot breeze off the fire ruffled my hair as I watched, and the column of smoke, which seemed almost lazy a moment ago, flattened into a haze.

Pack up, Ian said.

We scuttled down the hill to the lunch area and packed the trash, stuffing the excess food into the backpacks. Tendrils of smoke crossed the hilltop, through the crowns of the trees. A fine haze insinuated the glade, and two of the older men coughed. Black floating ashes carried on the wind settled into the high grass, followed by an ember still glowing at the edges. Where the ember settled near the top of the hill, the grass caught fire. Shocked at how quickly the situation had turned, we stared at the spot fire, uncertain what to do about it. I looked at Ian, but he shrugged.

Maybe we should just get out of here, he said.

Everyone was scurrying toward the trail when Albert shouted, Hold it! Hold it! We turned to him. Take this end! he said to one of the college men, and the two of them hauled the aluminum jug full of sweet iced tea toward the top of the hill. Catching on, I ran and caught the bottom. The spot fire was still no larger than a campfire when we arrived, but with the wind it would spread across the firebreak in minutes. Albert unscrewed the top of the jug, and the entire group heaved with a great communal grunt, upturning the jug, spilling the sweet iced tea onto the fire. We cheered. For the next few minutes everybody stamped on the embers, grinning at each other, and feeling powerful all out of proportion. Eventually, our elation died down and we trudged back the hill to the trail opening, dragging the aluminum jug behind us.

One by one, the others filed down the trail and disappeared into the trees. I was at the end of the line, and while the rest moved on, I turned for one last look at what we had done. A thick white haze rolled over the hillside, tendrils like root tips growing between the trees, the hillocks, the scattered boulders, the tufts of grass. The firebreak had been stripped of trees, the golden grass quivering in the new wind. The only tree left was the single fifteen-foot spruce I had left standing to spare the baby birds, and I said a quick prayer for their safety. The glade, the open firebreak, with the single tree became something more: a sense of new life, an ineffable presence in the devastation. The glade had become a sacrament, a sign of something hidden, sacred, as if the glade was the forest and the forest was the world and the world was through and through stuffed with God. I felt the ambiguity of the moment. We had to destroy this glade in order to save it. Death and life folded into each other, and in that folding, the world prickled with holiness. When the baby died, I asked, Who is this God? And here, standing in this glade, I had a peek at an answer, an answer that like the name of God, could not be spoken.

"Too late have I loved you!" Saint Augustine prayed. "And behold, you were within, and I apart." The entire world is a sacrament of God, tingling with divinity. The word "sacrament" is a Latin word, *sacramentum*, and it referred to an offering given at a temple during the signing of a contract, bringing gods to witness the act. Over the centuries, the idea mutated to refer to that ineffable dimension of all experience, where God is manifest in the symbolic power of ordinary experience. The world speaks to us of God, and we respond with yearnings we cannot put into words. There is something ancient about this part of us, something kneaded into the human psyche. Long before Homer, when the Greeks came to a place they felt was holy, they sensed it. They never asked, "Are we crazy?" They asked, "What god lives here?"

This is the same feeling I get when looking down on a deep Alpine valley, or under the trees in the play of twilight, or in a cathedral with one candle burning. When I have explored the silence, when I am purified, when I no longer live in and for my false self, when I am open to the world, and if I am in just the right place, and in just the right frame of mind, the world opens for me like a flower. This is the world as it really is, the ineffable truth beyond concepts, beyond rationality. Poets see it. Mystics see it, for their two worlds are deeply intertwined. So can we all.

We said good-bye, see ya, thanks for the help, and everyone headed in different directions—the college kids back to town, Beth waving, Ian and Albert and I back to the cabin. The weather had continued to change with the new front—storm clouds boiling from the southwest, lightning shivering inside. I prayed for rain.

Twelve

EVENING. A TIME FOR contemplation. A time for flight. Every bird in a hundred miles wheeled over the lake, and every bug swarmed around my head. The storm coming in loomed over the mountains, the clouds incandescent at the top, almost translucent, the whiteness sharp against the blue sky as if someone had stuck a million-watt lightbulb inside and switched it on. Lower down, the color deepened smoothly, ironclad and sullen, while in the distance, the clouds turned a dusty rose. At sunset, the storm towering over the mountains south of the lake turned golden amber, then rose, then red. Long after the sun had disappeared, and the rest of the world had darkened, the cloud bank glowed as if it had been charged with the sun and now ignited of its own. Lightning twitched inside and stabbed at the ground. The hills flashed into existence then winked out, the history of the universe compressed into nanoseconds. As night thickened, the world disappeared into darkness, hiding in its own shadow.

There is a Zen fable about a master and a student walking home in the rain, the world around them flashing on and off with the lightning. At home, the master told the student that for most people enlightenment was like the lightning—quick flashes of clarity, then back to darkness and ordinary life. Perhaps the human brain can handle only so much reality. Mine can't. I have had my moments of sudden clarity, the sense of a powerful presence, a feeling of unity, but the comings and goings of that feeling are a mystery to me and are out of my control. I can prepare for it, put myself in the way of it, but it appears of its own and leaves of its own. When it appears, it remains for ten minutes, a happy guest, or perhaps twenty, then fades. If I try to clutch at it, it vanishes altogether.

Contemplation, for Thomas Merton, is the highest human act—the spiritual life itself, its core, its heart. "It is spiritual wonder. It is spontaneous awe at the sacredness of life, of being. It is gratitude for life, for awareness and for being. It is a vivid realization of the fact that life and being in us proceed from an invisible, transcendent, and infinitely abundant Source." Here is where the differences between East and West become apparent. As systems of thought, Buddhism and Judeo-Christianity are the antipodes. They swim in opposite oceans, where the Coriolis forces of reality swirl in opposing directions. For Buddhism, the world is already One, unbreakable save by illusion, the sole division being between those who are asleep and those who are awake, those who live in illusion and those who have been enlightened. The spiritual life in Buddhism edges toward an awakening to the true facts of things, to the illusory nature of the world and of each thing in it, and finally to the illusory nature of the self. Enlightenment leads to freedom from suffering because suffering comes ultimately from trying to live out an illusion. Judaism and Christianity begin with a world already in division, a world of dualities—good and evil, life and death, heaven and hell, God and the world. These dualities are inherited from still older cultures, and are the grandchild of the West's belief in the reality of the physical world. Unity for western religion is built by effort, leading to a harmony of individuals rather than to a realization of an already existing unity. Buddhism can therefore do rather well without raising the question of God, and would prefer not to because doing so would put these ultimate questions into language, and that is an impossible task. Might as well stuff the sea into a pint bottle. Judeo-Christianity, on the other hand, cannot avoid the question of God; for God, in that universe, is the true fact of things. What is wonderful about the spiritual life is that for much of the way, these two vastly different systems can walk together, different as they are, swapping ideas back and forth like baseball cards. Thomas Merton, Thich Nhat Hanh, Raimundo Pannikar, and the Dalai Lama all see room for dialogue, and for the same reason—the spiritual life, for all its million faces, is much the same around the world, for the experience of silence is the same. The difference in thought creates a difference in flavor within the experience—one leading to self-realization, the other leading to the perfect relationship—but that only spices up the spiritual life even more.

For these reasons, I believe that the contemplative life is the only life worth living. It is lived by scientists and philosophers, monks and mystics alike. Contemplation is the deep glance, the awakening to a world with dimension, a world that blends with the Mystery, chock full, moment to moment, with significance. For those few moments, the experience answers all questions, shrinking their importance, as if seeing an elephant dwarfs all theories about elephants. In my life, contemplation has felt more like a turn, an unexpected shift in perception, without a change in hearing or seeing, but with an expansion of their meaning, as if the ceiling had folded back and opened to the sky. What I see or hear suddenly means more, becoming an instance of holiness. It is nothing like what people experience in drug hallucinations, and makes the artificial schizophrenia of LSD seem anemic. It is not a high, or a trip, or a psychedelic dream. I am not turned on or tuned in—the world is turned on, its mystic heart laid bare. Contemplation doesn't take me elsewhere; nor does it give me visions. I don't see flights of angels, or hear secret voices, but I see the ordinary world revealed. This does not require an actual alteration of perception, or an alteration of consciousness, but only a measure of stillness. I need only get out of my own way, attend, and make myself ready. This is not as easy as it sounds.

Certainly, there are people around who claim to have visions and who claim to hear voices. I cannot judge this experience, because it is theirs, not mine. I can only say that I get itchy when I'm around such people, because their experience is so different from my own. It sets them apart from the rest of the human race and makes them special. The experience I have had does not set me apart, because it is an ordinary human experience intensified. It is something that anyone can do, if they want to. It is our human heritage writ large. We are not the rational animal, or the wise animal; we are the contemplative animal.

One of the chief qualities of true contemplation is that, like the name of God, it cannot be spoken. I may say what the experience is like, or say how it might feel. People ask me, What is it like? and I stammer. I drool. I make attempts and each attempt grows ever more incoherent. I babble, they babble, we all babble together. Poetry helps, but every poet's poem is different, and the best any poet can do is to say, This is what it was like for me. Kind of. The way into contemplation is through silence, and any attempt to express that silence in language kills the silence. As soon as I talk about contemplation, I'm not contemplating anymore. I am speaking. I have walked away from contemplation, from the act itself, in order to go on safari for words. Language is not contemplation, it is description; contemplation is bigger than language. I can use words, symbols, images, concepts to hint at what I know in contemplation, but if I try to put that knowledge into clear language, I have to immediately unsay what I have just said. Language is a machine. It puts the world into boxes, into categories of object and action, and then links the boxes to make sentences. Contemplation is the opposite of this. Where language separates into reason, contemplation unites. Where language mediates, contemplation makes immediate. In contemplation, what I know is not a fact, or an argument, or a proof, or even a metaphor. It is not inside me. It is not something I possess. In contemplation, I am what I know.

The storm boiled through the night, but sadly without rain. At first, I sat on the porch and watched the show through the screen, but when it didn't rain, I taunted the storm and sat boldly on the aluminum chair near the floating dock. I wanted to be inside it, to be a part of it, the night and the storm, the lightning and the universe clicking on and off. Ecstasy is a near cousin to lunacy, and I did not know if what I felt at that moment was a state of mystical amazement or a state of dementia. I felt pulled out of myself, amazed, crushed, and elevated at the same time. I was full of wonder. Surely, I thought, a god must live in this place. The air crackled, boomed, grumbled, and flickered. The lakeside was charged with static electricity, a giant tesla coil; for three rolling seconds, the hair on the back of my head stood up, and my fingers and toes wanted to curl. My body had been positively charged for lightning to strike. Throughout the evening and far into the night, lightning branched from cloud to cloud, three or four spears at a time, then stabbed the earth, jumping, dancing on top of the mountains. The world was created ex nihilo and then destroyed, flickering black and then electric blue, off on off, as if God couldn't make up his mind whether to create the thing. Hour after hour, storm cells appeared from behind the mountains to the south, seared and crackled stately overhead, then passed on to the north, only to be followed by another.

When I was a child, I knew the ecstasy of storms. As one approached, my brothers and sisters and I, feeling the electric charge building, tied flannel sheets around our shoulders as flowing capes and ran wildly screaming into the wind, shouting Charge! and jumping over hedges, shooting one another with invisible bullets, and dying magnificently on the grass. The wind gathered, the storm broke, and our mother called us in to sit by the window and watch the show, the ecstasy bottled for a time until the storm passed. The energy leaked from us and we sat in chairs, subdued. Children and dogs. I have seen dogs bark at thunder, chase their tails, huddle shivering in the corner, then run from room to room, eyes shining with dog joy. As an adult, I have learned to keep this mania corralled, burying it under a flannel sheet of civilization. It would not do as a grown man to jump over hedges screaming every time a storm blows. I still feel it, though, that giddy excitement, that terror mixed with vitality, orphic and primal.

There has long been a fearful confusion about states of madness and states of contemplative ecstasy. Some reject mysticism as evil on this account, and call contemplation madness, and embrace a cold rationalism that gives no joy but feels safe.

A tree is known by its fruit, said Jesus. Truth is revealed by what it produces. The fruits of healthy contemplation are joy and peace of soul, an affirmation of life. Julian of Norwich, a fourteenth-century hermit nun, affirmed the goodness of life, even as people were dying all around her from plague. All will be well, she said, and all will be well. For contemplation is sweet, as the seventeenth-century Carmelite Brother Lawrence said. It is like "suckling at the breasts of God." This is a very medieval idea, the Motherhood of God, with the whole human race like children wrapped in her care.

When I was an undergraduate, before I even thought of a seminary, I was besotted with rationalism, an atheist on alternate Tuesdays, sniffing at prayer, and belittling anything religious as "that old stuff." I thought that contemplation was against reason itself, and that the more contemplative something was, the weirder it had to sound. Contemplatives had to talk like sixties hippies, so that everything they said would be like cosmic, man. During that time, I read Brother Lawrence, and when I reached the part about the breasts of God, I made a face and felt confirmed. A month later, however, I was driving across the desert and saw this comet, and everything changed. That night, I learned about contemplation from the inside—an intuition, a recognition, a perception of the truth. I do this every day just to get by and think nothing of it; I recognize, remember, have flashes of insight. I never have to reason explicitly, because I believe in my memory and my intuition. If I didn't,

I'd never leave the house. Certainly, this is not a modern kind of rationality, which is critical, grounded in doubt, seeking proof before belief. Intuition is ancient, primal, human epistemology at its geographic center. It is an older rationality, best judged not by its adherence to scientific principles, but by its results. A tree is known by its fruit.

The storm rolled overhead sometime late in the night, and I dragged myself off to bed. The next morning, sirens swelled from across the lake. Horns honked. I carried my binoculars out to the floating dock. A curl of smoke rose over the dry hill on the other side of the lake, even as the morning breeze picked up. A single fire engine sat on the highway at the bottom of the fire, red lights flashing, with more sirens coming west from Salmon Arm. A police car arrived, and another fire engine. I scurried back to the cabin, turned on the radio to glean some news. The announcer said that a new fire had started near the Trans-Canada Highway east of Chase, and that they were going to close the highway for the rest of the day. The day, according to the weatherman, would be hot and dry and windy.

Within an hour, the curl had become a veil. An hour after that, the veil had become a wall. The fire had quickly climbed up the hill and spread east with the morning wind. By eleven, Ian stopped by, climbed out of his truck, and sauntered cowboylike down to the floating dock. He stood beside me for a full three minutes, the two of us staring at the wall of smoke. Three new fire trucks arrived, and a helicopter circled around the fire. Another helicopter arrived from Kamloops, approached the top of the hill from the upwind side, and dropped fire retardant in the fire's path.

Ian and I decided to drive up to the mountain to see if they needed our help. By the time we crossed the bridge at Squilax, another helicopter had arrived, dropped its load, and was gone. We hit the highway and pulled over about a hundred feet from the police cars, their lights spinning and flashing like Las Vegas. The fire had already climbed halfway up the hillside by the time we arrived, and a line of young men and women in yellow shirts, slinging Pulaskis and chain saws over their shoulders, were worming up the hill about a hundred feet downwind from the fire. From where we stood, the fire roared constantly. Pumper trucks arced streams of water at the lower end of the hill, while helicopters dropped red retardant from up above. The fire roared, the wind caught embers and carried them over the tops of the trees eastward. A spot fire started near one of the crews, but they quickly stamped it out. Smoke filled half the sky, a dirty white-and-gray column that rose a hundred feet over the hill, then flattened, pulling eastward, stretching and thinning. Halfway up the hill, the fire crowned—bad news. Whole trees were aflame, blazing towers. One caught and exploded.

How's it going? Ian asked an officer.

Depends on who you ask. One guy over there says it's going just fine, as long as the wind doesn't pick up. Another guy says it's almost completely out of control, especially since the wind is going to come crashing through any time now. Take your pick.

Do they think they'll have it under control today?

The officer shook his head. No bloody way, he said. They haven't got the crew. Tomorrow, maybe, or the next. We'll have to open this road sometime soon, though. One way or the other, it's going to be a big show tonight for the cabin people, eh?

At that moment, a fire captain came over pointing and shouting, and shooed us off his mountain.

We arrived at the cabin twenty minutes later. At lunchtime, I slouched toward the kitchen, gathered cheese, mayonnaise, and a fresh loaf of Italian bread from the refrigerator, and set them on the counter. As I did so, the cabin door opened and Albert walked inside, followed by Joe.

Albert, I knew as soon as I opened up the refrigerator, you would show up, I said.

Yes, but this time I'm actually bringing food, Albert said, and set two bags of groceries onto the counter.

Well, well, I said, sticking my nose into one of the bags. What did you bring me?

Albert pulled things out of the bags—beer, Coke, white bread, processed meat, more beer. I bowed to him, gave him a beer and Joe a Coke. Wait, Albert said, as he twisted open his beer. We were in the Okanagan, and we got something special. He reached into the bag and pulled out a bag of pears. I washed one, sliced a slab off one end with a paring knife, and smiled. Fresh pear.

All is forgiven, Albert. This makes us even. Your debt for eating all my food is canceled.

Albert grinned. I never owed you nothing, white man.

Eating a pear with a knife is the most perfect form of contemplation there is—a world made for savoring: coolness, sweetness, texture, juice running down my chin. Sometimes I think of the world as a pear, spouting juice, sweetness inside and out. Every morning I take a bite and chew all day, swallowing finally in the evening, the perfect act of savoring—the taste, the smack, the tang, the zest of it, the sweetness on my tongue, the delicate odor, the sweet yellow-green of the skin, the curve in my hand. With the right attitude in mind, simply eating a pear can be erotic. Contemplation is the appreciation of everything that is as a gift from God—joy in the moment, God in the moment. This implies a collection of the senses, a gathering awareness of beauty, of the sublimity of time. The pear is a good, and the pleasure is a good, and in the sweet moment of eating, they form a prayer. The idea is never to let any momentary pleasure stand on its own, as a good to be pursued by itself, but as a sacrament, a sign of God's good presence, a sign that everything in the world, even my own soul, my own body, is a gift.

A parable:

Alexander the Great heard of a garden in the East where the Tree of Life grows, and anyone who ate its fruit would always be young and innocent. To own such a tree, Alexander said, he would conquer the world. When he became king, he crossed the Hellespont and destroyed the Persian army, cut the head of Xerxes from his shoulders, and set it on a pike.

Driving eastward, he rode into India, and the people there sent an emissary with a hundred servants to honor him. In saffron robes, they waited under a silk pavilion for him at the crossroads, one road leading to a marble city, the other east, over the mountains. There, they offered him spices, silver, and emeralds. They also praised him and sang epics about his conquests. All this time, Alexander said nothing. He never left his saddle, but when they were done, he questioned the emissary about the garden he had heard of, the earthly Paradise where the Tree of Life grows. The old man bowed, said yes he had heard of this place, but it was far to the east, over the mountains, near the palace of the emperor of the Middle Kingdom.

Alexander thanked him for his gifts, then left them lying in the road, for what were emeralds and silver compared to the Tree of Life? As his army disappeared over the foothills of the Himalayas, the emissary returned to his home. That afternoon, he laughed as he tended the pear tree in his garden, pruned the branches to let more fruit grow in the spring. How foolish the Westerners are, he said. There are thousands of magic gardens, ten thousand trees of life, a hundred thousand wonders in this world. But there is only one pear tree like *this*, with fruit so sweet.

There are two kinds of contemplation in Christian tradition, apaphatic and kataphatic. Apaphatic contemplation abandons all images, all words, and all formulas of prayer. It pares down mental noise by rejecting language and by refusing all ideas about God, all theology. It is the kind of Christian prayer closest to Zen. Kataphatic contemplation uses images, experiences, memories, stories, paintings, music, pears, beauty of any kind to put you into the right frame of mine, to make you aware of God at each moment, each second of the day. Kataphatic prayer is sacramental, finding God in each taste, each sight, each sound, finding God everywhere in the world. It does not try to approach God directly, but through creation, and assumes that the natural and the supernatural exist in continuity, that the profane, ordinary world shades into the divine, that the true reality is manifested in sign and symbol, in the sacramental presence of every good thing that exists. The sacred is not somewhere else, but here; the natural world is not debased, but is the vestibule of God. We are the bridge that joins the sacred with the profane, because even on our worst days, we carry a touch of divinity. Kataphatic prayer uses creation and images of creation, ideas, sensual experience, art, poetry, music, all to establish contemplative states. It sees each human experience, each human act except sin, as holy, because everything we are tingles with God.

Among the Desert Fathers, someone came by and asked an old man, "What do I need to do to be saved?" The old man was making rope, and he looked up from his work and said, "You're looking at it."

I finished the last of the pear, balanced the core on my chest, and sighed. Ian grinned at me from the other lounger, as if to say, You're easy to please. Joe had wandered down to the floating dock and sat in the aluminum chair, without moving, as still as the lake at dawn, and the thought flashed through my mind that he had died there, and that we would find him later in the afternoon with a smile on his face. Albert stood behind us, hands in the pockets of his jeans, and stared across the lake toward the fire. He seemed unmoving, with worry in his eyes. I realized then that he, too, was watching Joe.

That old man, Albert said. I found him on the floor this morning, passed out. And will he go into hospital?

You want us to take him? Ian said. We could all go.

Albert shook his head. When I told him he should go, he just laughed. Says now he wants to come here and watch the fire.

That's why I'm here, Ian said.

What do you want to do about Joe? I said to Albert, not wanting to be sidetracked. Ian never liked to talk about sick people.

Albert shrugged with his hands still in his pockets. That old man's too stubborn. He won't go. Won't say anything else.

Albert meandered down to the lakeshore and sat on the pebble beach next to Joe's chair. For about five minutes, Joe didn't move, didn't seem to acknowledge Albert's presence, until one hand dropped off the armrest of the chair and lightly touched Albert's shoulder, and then returned. A twin-engine tanker plane with orange-and-black stripes on the wings and the tail flew in over the lake, then climbed up over the fire, dropping red rain from its belly. I knew that somewhere in there was the answer I had been looking for, about why the baby had to die, but the only thing I could say was that in the midst of life and in the midst of death, the presence of God was always there, if I was willing to look, and whenever I encountered that presence, I would find joy and peace of soul. That is the answer, I suppose, the kind of answer that makes sense only in the finding, not in the telling. Even Job, after he had heard the voice of God in the whirlwind, said: "I put my hand over my mouth. Though I have spoken once, I will not do so again."

We passed the day watching the pillars of smoke rising from the mountain. Ian went out for steaks, and we barbecued a massive dinner. Joe, white and sickly, left his untouched. Ian methodically worked his way through several helpings, then reached out and forked up Joe's steak. Albert watched him and puffed out his cheeks. Joe began to hum a hymn I hadn't heard since childhood, and I filled in the words in my mind.

Beati mortui in Domino morientes
Beati mortui in Domino morientes
Blessed are the dead who die in the Lord
Blessed are the dead who die in the Lord

Don't you go die on me, old man, Albert said softly.

You're a good boy, Albert, Joe said.

By seven, we had finished eating and cleaned the dishes. Ian whistled as he brushed the grill and put away the rest of the food in his truck. I walked with him down to say good-bye to Albert and Joe, then followed him back to the cars. You let me know how the old man is doing, eh? he said, frowning. I nodded, shook his hand, and waved as he backed up the drive and onto the dirt road above.

The evening wandered into night. The fire burned away across the lake, with Cold War–vintage cargo planes and World War II bombers skimming the lake, rising, turning at the hillside, dropping, then turning west for another load. Rotating beacons flashed from the fire trucks gathered on the highway, while police cars sped in and sped out, lights and sirens making way. As the night deepened, the fire stood out against the darkness, the red glow flickering, as if the face of God had been carved into the hill. Medieval alchemists claimed that God made fire first, the subtlest element of all, the most lively, the most undefined, and the most uncontrollable. Fire is the element of change, substance to substance, element to element. To watch fire is to watch creation happening, that which raises mountains and moves the clouds, that which forms stars and destroys them, that which gives life and causes death.

A few minutes later, I pulled the boat motor into life, cast off and growled out toward the far side of the lake, the loons scattering as I approached, the bats whizzing over my head, plucking midges out of the air. I peeled a pear and ate it, strip by strip. When I dropped anchor, I thought that I would be alone out there, a hundred feet offshore, but soon there was a gathering of small boats, people from cabins up and down the shore, people from Chase, even a boat or two from Scotch Creek. We seemed to cluster together, as if to reassure ourselves in the night.

There is something about a fire that stirs contemplation. Sitting in front of a fire, anything can happen. The world spins on, and we with it. The world catches fire at supersonic speed; it smolders, hidden. The world is a banked fire, ashes on top, coals glowing red underneath. I breathed a prayer for Joe and the rising of his soul, and for his flesh burning away with age and something in his brain. Plane after plane skimmed the water, strobe lights flashing on their wings, landing lights, rotating beacons, all aflame. The wings, fuselage, and tail were dark, so it looked as if the lights themselves were flying down the lake and over the hills, dropping red rain. I breathed a prayer for Albert, and one for Ian, and one for the baby's mother, the father, the baby itself. I breathed a prayer for Mrs. Mouncy and for Nora Cooper. I breathed a prayer for the whole world, living and dead, present now in this moment. Another plane flew over the lake, invisible behind its own landing lights, engines roaring, bearing down, closer and closer, then pulling away overhead, an old C-119 Packet that flashed into being in the glare of the fire, and with its passing suddenly God was there, mystery upon mystery. All that night, the fire burned, and all that night the planes flew. All that night, the fire trucks flashed, and policemen appeared and disappeared. The flames on the hillside seemed suddenly like magma bursting out of the earth, a hidden fire erupting, the same fire that filled everything and everyone. Like the bush that burned and was not consumed, the world was full of flame. The fire burned away all my worries, all my desires. I watched the fire burn the world and said, All will be well, all will be well.

IV
The Fourth Circle of Silence
EMBRACING ALL

HOW TO WEAR A HAT

Take my hat, a homburg or a panama,
black or white, a hat full of stars.
Roll it on your head, front to back;
give a tilt for sport.
Smooth its edge with a thumb and finger.
Flick the brim.
Turn this way, that way, in the glass.
Regard yourself,
your dash, your air, your style.

Now find a lamp by some dark street
past twelve, where night's people
nightly strut their stuff.
Curl your mouth in absolution.
Forgive them everything.
Nod your head; wink.
Learn to wear a hat as God wears the world.

JAMES A. CONNOR

Thirteen

THE ROOM IS DARK; moonlight pools on the floor beside my chair, the clutter on the desk is half in moonshine, half in shadow, ghostly, like old memories. I come to this office late at night to stare out the window and remember twenty years back, to the retreat at the cabin that opened wounds and healed wounds. So many changes, and yet the same presence, the same Mystery, life folded into life. Lightning flashes and the shadow of God is revealed in the world, like a face on a wall. Sometimes, walking in the warm sun, a mile or two and suddenly I turn a corner, into a forest glade, come upon a bit of stream. I walk into the city to a street corner and find God there, too intimate, too close to touch, and all I can do is smile like the Buddha. I put my hand out like a blind man wanting to feel a beam of light, and too quickly it is gone. I walk through the city; people pass by, rushing on errands, on business; they open cell phones, and rush away. Suddenly, God, too, is there, then gone. I wander into Starbucks, order a tall coffee, extra cream, and a little hard biscuit with one end chocolate; I sit at a table near the window, bathing in the sun, remembering the moment, knowing that though I cannot feel it, the presence is there, behind that thin curtain, that chiffon veil of the world. I remember the heat, the satisfaction, the joy that hits when I turn that corner, tumbling twenty years back to that night sitting in a boat watching a fire storm on a hillside, and knowing, all outside of reason: God is here.

I finally left the Jesuits for so many reasons, because of loneliness and because of the storm of other people's lives. Finally, it wasn't really my place. I stopped trying to tell people who God is because I figured that God is beyond all telling. The rest they would have to find out for themselves. There was a conversion in this, a turning away from the simple words and easy dogmas of my childhood in order to cling to the Mystery. I am a Catholic today because it is a good way for me to be. It is my path to God, though it isn't for everyone. You practice a religion because you find God there—no other reason. No one can explain his or her path, nor do they need to. Mine is as peculiar as anybody's, I suppose. Besides, I like the poetry.

I thought I would learn some deep profound thing, something cryptic I could puzzle over, like a literary critic reading *Finnegan's Wake.* What I learned was something simpler, so basic it at first seems banal. When I embrace God, I embrace life; when I embrace life, I embrace God. I embrace life moment to moment, day to day, accepting each good day, pain and suffering included, as it comes. Life is paradox and mystery. I have learned to accept paradox, to call it my home, and to call life good, sometimes in spite of the evidence. We grew up in a century that has seen thousands of African Americans hanged on trees. We grew up in a century that has seen millions of Jews, Gypsies, and Poles tortured, gassed, burned in ovens, murdered on an assembly line. We grew up in a century that has seen Armenians, Cambodians, Serbs, Croatians, and Muslims killed by the millions. We grew up in a century that has seen famine in Africa, that continent of sorrow, where AIDS gathers to depopulate whole nations. We grew up in a century of war, hunkering down under desks, waiting for the bombs to fall. What else can we do but embrace the Mystery? It would be easy to listen to Job's wife, to curse God and die, to surrender to horror, and to ignore that holy fire at the heart of the world, but to do this would be to give up on life itself. To embrace life, we accept both suffering and joy. We affirm the truth found in silence; we find God whirling at the center of the universe. Anyone who encounters God acknowledges that life is good and ultimately full of joy.

In 1654, Blaise Pascal, mathematician and scientist, met God. It changed his life. He wrote about it in a short passage, his memorial, that he scribbled onto a scrap of paper and pinned inside his clothes, keeping it secret until his death, when his friends found it as they prepared him for burial. On it, he wrote:

The year of Grace, 1654,
Monday, November 23rd, feast of St. Clement, Pope and Martyr, and others in the martyrology.
The vigil of St. Chrysogonus, martyr, and others.
From about half past ten at night until about half past midnight,

FIRE

GOD of Abraham, GOD of Isaac, GOD of Jacob
not of the philosophers and of the scholars.
Certainty. Certainty. Consciousness. Joy. Peace.
GOD of Jesus Christ
My God and your God.
Your GOD will be my God.
Forgetting the world and all else save God.
He is only found by the ways taught in the Gospel.
Greatness of the human soul.
Righteous Father, the world has not known you, but I have known you.
Joy, joy, joy, tears of joy.

This is true mysticism, transcending human action. No one can make it happen. It comes of its own, for those who receive it, and cannot be denied as was Jacob Marley as a bit of undigested beef or a piece of underdone potato. It is not a hallucination, and no drug can induce it.

Its heart is conversion, a change of life, and yet a return to life. The mystic does not understand God anymore than she ever did, because understanding implies control, and control is to speak the name of God. Nevertheless, there is a certainty to it, the certainty of immediate experience, bypassing the weaknesses of the senses. She finds that God is beyond all categories, all attempts at description, that God is neither male nor female, neither mother nor father, neither black nor white. God is not an old man with a long, white beard, sitting on a cloud, looking like a guitarist for ZZ Top. God is not an earth mother nor a sky father. God is personal and not personal, a mind and not a mind. Oddly enough, the Buddhists are right—there is no God, at least not as we have imagined God. Oddly enough, the Christians are right—there is a God, and we speak to that God every day. I cannot collapse these opposites; I can only say that in some mysterious way, there is no difference between them. The rest, I will pass over in silence. Few people have ever experienced this God, and those who have have suffered much before and after. Most of us work out our spiritual lives in uncertainty and darkness, with flashes of lightning that illuminate the world. I am content. Perfect union with God is up to God, and not up to me. And so, I go on slogging.

Modern life doesn't prepare us for this loss of control. We are raised to make things happen, not to let things happen, and nothing gets in the way of the spiritual life like the urge to control. This does not mean that spirituality is passive, because the spiritual life requires work—hard work. Active contemplation is the art of silence, the life of prayer, where each soul focuses attention on the presence of God. I breathe, take in air, and God is in the breathing. I feel the sun on my face, and God is in the warmth. God radiates from every glass of water, from every blade of grass. God plays hide-and-seek in the night, in the half-light of the moon and in the shadows it makes. As the Koran says: To God belong the East and West; and wherever you turn, there is the Face of

God. This turning to find the Face of God is active contemplation; it is active because I am doing it. I focus my attention on the world to open my eyes to the mystery. It is an art, the root of all art, the contemplative gaze mastered by poets and painters, the contemplative hearing mastered by composers, the contemplative touch, the contemplative smell, the contemplative taste. You can eat the world as painters eat the world, dance with the universe as if it were all music.

For those who are blessed, or perhaps cursed, with passive contemplation, God moves into their lives and rewrites the code. Like Saint Paul blasted off his horse on the Damascus Road, they are grabbed, shaken, changed about, whirled as in a tornado, and they are never the same. I say they are blessed because the experience is the most exquisitely beautiful anyone could ever have, the Beatific Vision on earth, Dante's Mystical Rose while still in the flesh. I say they are cursed because their lives almost always move onto strange paths, out of comfortable middle-class homes like Saint Francis, and into the poorest hovels, or they take to the roads as wandering pilgrims, or they retreat into monasteries and live forever in silence. Such people are rare, though. Most of us find God in the nanoseconds, in the flashes of lightning, in the space between one breath and the next. Most of us are chosen to live a more ordinary kind of life, a twilight life where visions of God flicker on and off.

The silent life is the first step to contemplation. It is the one door into communion with God. It leads to insight about the world, true insight about the nature of existence. Silence alone teaches. Go and sit in your cell and it will teach you everything.

There's nothing like a forest fire to interrupt your reading. The fire across the lake lasted for two more days, while I sat on the floating dock, shoes off, feet in the water, feeling like Huckleberry Finn, watching the silver trout circling my legs. The stack of books I had brought with me grew, and though I swore I would read every one, I was restless. I started one, read a couple of pages, then started another. All the while, I kept an eye on the fire as air tankers lined up, dropped a load, and circled back to town. After the fire had crowned, burning away the tops of the trees, it spread, hopping east to the streambed, then over to the next hill. Fire crews crawled up the hillside, stamping out infant fires before they could mature. I watched the hill from across the lake, peering through binoculars. Now and then, a trout leaped and I actually *saw* the day, and breathing, nearly made the turn into Mystery. I felt the presence in the burning, but then it faded, or I pulled away. All day the feeling of presence remained, tangled at the edges of my thoughts. *Fire.* It tingled, called, seduced. Three times that afternoon, I relaxed, breathed, made the turn, and waited. *Fire.* The last time, it erupted inside me, a molten touch that was gone at once. Joy and peace. Joy. Tears of joy.

Ian arrived later that day, stood on the dock, watched the fire, chatted a bit, then left. Albert drove by with Joe in his car, told me he was taking the old man to the hospital. I hobbled up barefoot to Albert's car and leaned in the window. Joe's face was white, a shadow of death in his eyes.

You get well, Joe, I said. That's an order.

Joe grinned and shrugged.

Albert's hands shook. You want me to come with you? I said to him.

He shook his head sadly. No, he said. Whole family's going to be there. It'll be okay.

You let me know.

Albert nodded and started his car. I watched them back up the drive and wondered if I would ever see Joe again. I waved, and Joe waved back. When they were gone, gloom condensed around me like a morning fog. I felt as if I had suddenly lost my sight, for the presence retreated with the mood, my attention cut into pieces. Fretting about Joe, I stayed in the darkness for two days and waited for news. The fire crew took control of the fire in that time, but I hardly noticed. Then they opened the highway. I prayed, read, watched the lake; the fire inside me cooled to ashes. Around four in the afternoon of the second day, a car pulled into the drive, and I turned half around on the dock, hoping it was Albert with news. It was Nora Cooper, actually driving a car. Mrs. Mouncy sat in the passenger seat across from her, the perpetual cigarette hanging out the side of her mouth.

Howdy, Nora, Ma, I said, as the two of them walked toward the dock.

Ma stood over me and leaned down. Go home! she said. She straightened and flicked her half-smoked cigarette into the water.

You drove all the way out here just to tell me that?

Go home, Ma said. We want the cabin.

Oh? Girls night out? Big party? Nora hid her mouth behind her hand. Ma snorted, and I knew then that I wasn't far wrong. You *are* having a party! I said.

Ma crossed her arms, then lit a new cigarette. Puffing, she tried to look prim. Some ladies are coming out tonight, she said. Tomorrow, we're going to clean the cabin.

It'll take me a while to pack, I told Ma.

That's all right, as long as you're out of here by dark. We don't want any men around.

Oh, I said. Evil rites in the forest. Dead cats. Eye of newt.

No, Nora said conspiratorially. Beer, cigarettes, and gossip.

That's what I like to see, I said. Christianity at its best! Nora snickered, then smiled at me Britanically. Quite, she said.

Looking back on those events as from a twenty-year height, time shifts and memories flutter like birds. A year and a half after the retreat, before I left Canada for good, I celebrated Ash Wednesday in a packed church. Candles, incense, and ashes. A terribly earnest woman, with short, dark, nunlike hair, strummed a guitar almost as big as she was, while her husband supported her on a string bass. Twice, she chided us about picking up the tempo. Catholics can turn "Stars and Stripes Forever" into a dirge. Now and then their son showed up with his drum set, but thankfully not that day. The last member of the group was a willowy blond girl with a sweet soprano, who showed up to sing and then disappeared as soon as Mass was over. I suspected she was a closet Anglican. Throughout the church, people stuffed themselves into pews, with fifty more leaning against the back wall, because Ash Wednesday is always a hit.

Funny how people who don't go to church for anything else show up for Ash Wednesday. There is a primal tug in the feast, a resonance that calls to people even when nothing else does. People held babies. People shushed toddlers. People walked beside great-grandmothers on uncertain feet. Only half of them went to Communion, but then after Mass, at the time for ashes, they lined up, hair combed, heads bowed, filling the aisles, all coming to receive the sign. They came up two by two, and I dipped my thumb into a crystal bowl full of ashes made from last year's Palm Sunday palms, and smeared a tiny cross on each forehead.

Remember that you are dust and unto dust you shall return, I said.

A businessman came, received his ashes, made the sign of the cross, and moved away. A grandmother came, held upright by a young boy, received her ashes, her lips moving silently, her rosary turning in her fingers. The boy leaned over and got his smear. Then Ian showed, and I was surprised, because I knew he wasn't Catholic, but I crossed him anyway.

Remember that you are dust and unto dust you shall return, I said.

Somewhere in there, Albert appeared, shot me a wicked grin, and I crossed him too. Mrs. Mouncy, Nora Cooper, Gordie the Mountie, a nurse from the hospital, Eddie Sokalski's mom.

Remember that you are dust and unto dust you shall return.

A tall, wide man in cowboy boots appeared. I crossed him, and when he moved aside, there she was behind him, holding her second child, an infant girl with a swirl of dark fuzz on her head, a tiny girl named Paulette. Her husband was behind her, and seeing them, I stopped. Thoughts and memories of the first child, so horribly crushed, hung around us like cobwebs, but then she held the new baby up and smiled, and we all smiled together. The new baby had been born three weeks before and baptized in their hometown. I never thought to see them again. She stepped forward and I drilled my thumb into the ashes, drew as perfect a cross as I could across her forehead.

Remember that you are dust and unto dust you shall return.

She smiled a quick smile, then held her baby up. The baby's face was red and still wrinkled, with miniature hands making fists over her chest, and the smell of new life wafting about her. I drew the tiniest cross I could manage, while she smiled, tears shining in her eyes, and her husband grinned over her shoulder.

Remember that you are dust and unto dust you shall return, I said. They moved aside, and I never saw them again in this life. Strands of memory from the year before coalesced as I stood distributing ashes. I said a quick prayer for Joe, as I had every day since his death. The memories came, faster and faster.

Joseph is in hospital, Nora said. I was gathering my things in the cabin, rolling my sleeping bag, and stuffing shirts, socks, pants, shoes into the duffel. Nora sat on the edge of the porch lounger, knees together, always a lady.

I know, I said. They stopped by on their way. I've been in a funk about the whole thing.

Nora sighed, looked away to the lake. A long time ago, she said, Joe decided he wanted to be close to God, and he was. He hardly said a word for thirty years, but everyone could see it anyway.

He set that fire, Ma said from the other room.

Nora didn't respond.

How blessed are the poor in spirit, I said. For theirs is the Kingdom of Heaven.

Amen, Nora said, and then we were silent for a while, until Nora broke it. He had a stroke, she said suddenly, looking at me. A few hours after he registered. He's in a coma now. Albert's with him.

I figured. I suppose I'd better get ready to do a funeral.

I spent the next half hour gathering shoes from under furniture, my toothbrush, the last of my Cokes. I left the beer for the ladies. I kissed Nora on the cheek and waved at Ma—she didn't like to be hugged—hauled my duffel and sleeping bag to the car, and backed up to the road. It was over. I was ready to face the world, one way or another. On the way out, I crossed the bridge at Squilax, pulled my car off to the edge of the highway across from the burned-out area, and got out to investigate. Most of the firefighters had already gone, the helicopters, the air tankers, the pumpers, the police, the lines of yellow-shirted fire crew. A fire inspector's car was parked on the other side of the road, and I could see him wandering over the hill, turning smoking logs with a Pulaski and hunkering down over a blackened mound of something. Skittering across the highway, I followed the streambed up the hill, plodding up about halfway. The inspector looked at me, then returned to his work, shaking his head.

Blackened tree skeletons poked into the air, a line drawing of a forest. Here and there, smoke curled out of the side of a tree, or out from under a rock. I stumbled over a black mound I thought was a stone, but it was the carcass of a deer. A hundred feet farther uphill, I came on a smoking pile of sticks, with the remains of an eagle, the smell of charred feathers in the air. The bird lay next to what might have been a nest with two blackened lumps that might have been chicks. The world had been boiled away, reduced to nothing. Turning, I climbed the side of the hill, wanting distance from the dead. At the top, I stood looking out over a blackened valley to the sunset, the sun dipping behind the crest of mountains, blue black in the distance. In minutes, the sun had dropped behind, and in that instant, the world balanced between day and night. Then it pinked, turned a dusky rose, a change that rolled across the hills like a tidal wave from the sea. The mountaintops, the valleys, the lake, the charred trees, the dead, seared land turned rose, the color of the angels, the color of the morning and the evening. The mystical fire still burned, the Mystery at the heart of the world, death and life folded into each other. And there, on the far side, was God.

More Books to Read

Spiritual Reading

Bennett-Goleman, Tara. *Emotional Alchemy: How the Mind Can Heal the Heart.* Foreword by the Dalai Lama (New York: Harmony Books, 2000).

Chopra, Deepak. *How to Know God: The Soul's Journey into the Mystery of Mysteries* (New York: Three Rivers Press, 2000).

Hanh, Thich Nhat. *Being Peace* (Berkeley: Parallax Press, 1996).

Kisly, Lorraine. *Ordinary Graces: Christian Teachings on the Interior Life.* Introduction by Philip Zaleski (New York: Bell Tower, 2000).

Merton, Thomas. *New Seeds of Contemplation* (New York: New Directions Press, 1961).

———et al. *The Asian Journal of Thomas Merton* (New York: New Directions Press, 1975).

Mitchell, Stephen, trans. *Bhagavad Gita: a New Translation.* (New York: Harmony Books, 2000).

Memoirs

Beck, Martha. *Expecting Adam: A True Story of Birth, Rebirth, and Everyday Magic* (New York: Crown Publishers, 1999).

Grohs-Martin, Silvia. *Silvie* (New York: Welcome Rain, 2000).

McCourt, Malachy. *A Monk Swimming* (New York: Hyperion Books, 1998).

About the Author

James A. Connor teaches at Kean University in New Jersey. A former Jesuit, he lives now on top of the Pocono Mountains with his wife, Beth, two border collies, and three cats. He is currently working on a second spiritual memoir.